KU-510-121

41

The Fabian Society

1   ...nk and
F   LIBRARY AND LEARNI...   ...eas and policy
debates ....ogressive politics.

With over 300 Fabian MPs, MEPs, Peers, MSPs and AMs, the Society
plays an unparalleled role in linking the ability to influence policy
debates at the highest level with vigorous grassroots debate among our
growing membership of over 7000 people, 70 local branches meeting
regularly throughout Britain and a vibrant Young Fabian section
organising its own activities. Fabian publications, events and ideas
therefore reach and influence a wider audience than those of any
comparable think tank. The Society is unique among think tanks in
being a thriving, democratically-constituted membership organisation,
affiliated to the Labour Party but organisationally and editorially
independent.

For over 120 years Fabians have been central to every important
renewal and revision of left of centre thinking. The Fabian commitment
to open and participatory debate is as important today as ever before
as we explore the ideas, politics and policies which will define the next
generation of progressive politics in Britain, Europe and around the
world. Find out more at **www.fabians.org.uk**

Northern College
Library

NC04614

CANCELLED

Fabian Society
11 Dartmouth Street
London SW1H 9BN
www.fabians.org.uk

Policy Report
Editorial Director: Tom Hampson
Pamphlet editor: Hannah Jameson

First published 2007

ISBN 978 07163 3061 5

This pamphlet, like all publications of the Fabian Society, represents not the collective views of the Society but only the views of the author. The responsibility of the Society is limited to approving its publications as worthy of consideration within the Labour movement. This publication may not be reproduced without express permission of the Fabian Society.

British Library Cataloguing in Publication data.
A catalogue record for this book is available from the British Library.

Printed and bound by Bell & Bain, Glasgow

Born Unequal
Why we need a progressive pre-birth agenda

by Louise Bamfield

About the author

Louise Bamfield is a Senior Research Fellow at the Fabian Society. From March 2004 to 2006, she was the lead researcher on the Fabian Commission on Life Chances and Child Poverty, chaired by Lord Victor Adebowale, which investigated some of the many ways in which poverty and disadvantage impact on children's life chances. She co-authored the Commission's final report, *Narrowing the Gap*, and its interim report, *Life Chances: What does the public really think about poverty?* From Spring 2007 she will lead a Fabian research project exploring ways to narrow the gaps in educational outcomes. She has a doctorate from the University of Cambridge in the philosophy of education.

Acknowledgments

The Fabian Society and authors are grateful to the Barrow Cadbury Trust and Bliss, the premature baby charity, for their generosity and willingness to support independent research. As with all Fabian Society publications, the content remains solely the responsibility of the author. The support of the partner does not imply endorsement of the views or recommendations contained in the research or report.

The author would like to thank all those who have contributed their time and expertise to the project, including Pandora Busch, Alison Hosie, Rachael Jolley, Alana McVerry, Agnes Munday and Liz Young at the Tarner Children's Centre, Jasmin Quereshi, Michael Reiss, Emily Robinson, Hazel Rutland, Peter Selman, Suzanne Speak and Kaye Surcouf. Particular thanks to all the women who kindly gave up their time to take part in our focus group discussions.

Contents

Born Unequal

Introduction

Born unequal

Britain is born unequal. Lying side by side in hospital wards, not yet a day old, babies already have very different chances of doing well at school, of getting a well-paid job, being healthy or ill, of going to university or to prison. If we are committed to tackling inequality in Britain, then social justice must begin before birth.Inequality at birth in Britain today is a stark matter of life and death. A child born to working-class parents is twice as likely to die before its first birthday. A single mother on income support is nine times more likely than most to experience a stillbirth. These inequalities in the distribution of life itself are linked to the opportunities and outcomes we experience in life; babies born with a low birth-weight are less likely to enjoy good health.

Some fairly modest changes in the way we support pregnant women and maternal health would save lives and reduce the risks some babies face. Bigger changes would take more time and money, and would raise broader questions about how our society is organised. But they could begin to break down the way in which advantages and disadvantages in life are passed down the generations. We have the choice as to whether to pursue them or not – and perhaps it will be easier to look away.

What should be clear is that the scale of inequalities at birth which we currently experience in Britain today are indefensible from any point on the democratic political spectrum. It does not matter, in this regard, whether you are a meritocrat of the centre-right or an egalitarian of the left: you should surely find much common cause, before you begin to disagree about broader visions of our society later on. If the concept of a fair society has substantive meaning, it must be one in which the circumstances of our birth, and the advantages and disadvantages which we inherit, matter much less than they do today. Now that social justice has, however recently, become a slogan to which all major political parties lay claim, the credibility test to be put to each party should be how they propose to reduce the gaps in life chances. This report recommends that each major party should develop its own serious agenda to narrow inequalities at birth.

There is strong evidence that the 'early years' agenda, pursued by Labour since 1997, must begin earlier. And a new pre-birth policy agenda is already emerging. Gordon Brown's decision to begin paying child benefit before birth – from 2009 it will be paid from the 29th week of pregnancy – responded to evidence put by the Fabian Life Chances Commission and other campaigners showing that low income was a significant factor in whether some pregnant women could afford the diet they needed.

This move has symbolic significance. It opens the door to a new policy and political debate: what more should Government do, across the next parliament, if it is to adopt a comprehensive strategy to narrow inequalities at birth?

This is a 'next decade' policy agenda, rooted in the best tradition of egalitarian thought. It renews the founding cause of the political left, yet, it is also an argument to throw down the gauntlet to all who lay claim to the mantle of social justice, across the political spectrum. As Tawney wrote, "While ... natural endowments differ profoundly, it is the mark of a civilised society to aim at eliminating such inequalities as have their source, not in individual differences, but in its own organisation." A fairer and more equal Britain would be less drab and less uniform, because it would be one in which more talent, more aspirations, more dreams were fulfiled – and fewer ambitions for ourselves and our children were wasted.

The challenge for the parties

This is an important opportunity to extend the politics of social justice, but we should be clear too about the danger of it being missed. Each of the major political parties will face significant difficulties in getting this agenda right.

Firstly, this Labour Government must prove that it has not reached the limits of the social progress which it is capable of making. Its quiet but persistent efforts to chip away at poverty and inequality have brought significant, and underrated, progress. But it has not yet found the confidence or language to communicate the vision which lies behind these strategies. Competing priorities for public resources will mean the chance of progress is slim unless we mobilise greater public support.

The Government's attack on child poverty, the creation of Sure Start and child trust funds, are animated by a concern about unequal life chances, which sees an equal start and fair chances in life as a defining missions for progressive politics. The pre-birth agenda should build on this. However, there is a risk that it could be significantly undermined by another prominent and more punitive public narrative around children; that of anti-social behaviour and the politics of 'respect'. Last Autumn's *Action Plan on Social Exclusion* dramatised these difficulties, as the case for more support for the most vulnerable children was drowned out by headlines about 'Baby Asbos'.

Punitive language may lose Labour the vital support of progressive constituencies who should support early interventions as an important tool in narrowing inequalities but instead, end up opposed to sinister 'social engineering'.

On the political right, the language of social justice and relative poverty is now being accepted and used. That is an important achievement for the Labour Government. Converting political enemies opens up progressive space, by shifting the political centre ground and removing once mainstream objections to the margins. If this 'politics of equality' takes root on the right, it will also open up a new argument between left and right, about the causes and consequences of inequality, and the means to narrow them. Yet, to date, the right's focus has been on a punitive discourse of individual responsibility for social circumstances.

Hard questions remain if the right wants to show that its commitment to social justice is real rather than rhetorical. It needs to answer the charge that its renewed focus on 'social responsibility', rather than the state, will not in practice equate to an abdication of governmental responsibility for outcomes. The Conservative Party has yet to offer much acknowledgement – still less a convincing analysis – of why inequality grew so sharply in the 1980s, but the central lesson is surely that the policies of governments do matter a lot.

The 'inequalities at birth' agenda also presents an important test of Liberal Democrat credentials on social justice. Intellectually, the reassertion of both market liberal and left-libertarian strands on the party's right and left may mean that the progressive social justice tradition – the New Liberalism which pioneered a more active and interventionist state in the early twentieth century – is in retreat.

The Liberal Democrats' current policies do not meet the redistribution test, with a significant bias in its priorities for public spending in favour of the middle classes rather than the poor, and a focus on older rather than young people. A commitment to the inequalities at birth agenda would be a significant step towards appealing to the altruism, and not the self-interest, of the progressive voters they are targeting.

If progressive politicians are to champion this agenda, they will also want to know whether this can meet the electoral test: could the marginal voters needed to win elections be convinced? Making the case for a fair chance in life and a decent start for all children should not be impossible. Indeed, these are issues that animate politics and its relevance to voters at the nursery school gates. Fabian deliberative opinion research on inequality and poverty has shown that, once there is evidence that acting makes a difference, you are no longer simply tugging at people's heart-strings. Instead, they can see the economic case – that investing in children and their futures is money well spent and avoids the bills on social failure later on.[1]

We need a generational political shift on the scale achieved by Attlee's welfare settlement, or Thatcher on the role of the market. Progressive pre-birth politics can only be sustained if it eventually becomes common ground between major parties, but we are a long way from that happening yet. Labour must make this an issue of contention between the parties and win the public argument to make that possible.

Box 1: What does 'life chances' mean?

This pamphlet builds on the Fabian Society's work on life chances, particularly the work of the Fabian Commission on Life Chances and Child Poverty.

The idea of life chances refers to the likelihood of someone achieving a range of important outcomes throughout the course of his or her life. In Britain, children born in different social and economic circumstances have very different chances of achieving certain important outcomes at particular stages of life, outcomes that impact upon their well-being, prospects and quality of life. In particular, children from disadvantaged backgrounds have systematically worse chances than their more fortunate peers in a range of areas – from infant mortality rates and cognitive development to educational outcomes, subsequent access to higher education and jobs, and life expectancy. By the time they are six years old, for example, children from disadvantaged backgrounds who demonstrated higher ability as infants have been overtaken by children from more affluent backgrounds who demonstrated lower ability.

Who a child's parents are and where she is born is still central in determining her chances in life. This offends against fundamental principles of fairness. Specifically, a child's life chances are shaped significantly by social fortune, the distribution of which is morally arbitrary. Tackling such undeserved and systematic inequalities is therefore a matter of social justice.

Of course, the fact that two people experience different outcomes is not in itself evidence of injustice. Factors such as individual choices, talent and luck and will affect their chances differently even when they come from very similar backgrounds. However, these factors alone clearly cannot explain why there are systematic differences in outcomes between different social groups.

This does not mean that a child's background determines the outcomes in his or her life – some people do of course go on to achieve positive outcomes despite disadvantageous beginnings. But background is key in determining one's *chances* of achieving such outcomes. The life chances approach focuses on risk factors – the factors which mean that people from certain groups face a higher risk of achieving poor outcomes than their more fortunate peers. This approach therefore allows us to move past the objection that 'some people make it nonetheless' to a focus on the obstacles people from certain social groups commonly face in their lives.[1]

The life chances approach offers a vision is of a society where children have more equal chances of achieving decent outcomes as they progress through life. Although it is difficult to imagine the gap in people's life chances will ever completely disappear, it is within our power to ensure the distribution of life chances is more equal.

1 | Life chances before birth

Our starting point in this pamphlet is a body of evidence that has been accumulating over recent decades of the importance of the period before birth in shaping future life chances. The extent of foetal development is an important predictor of a range of outcomes in each of the three major domains of child development: health, cognitive ability and emotional and social behaviour.

More specifically, birth weight, on which we focus here, is a key marker of the extent of foetal development. Low birth weight not only increases an infant's risk of mortality, but increases an infant's chances of experiencing developmental problems, such as low IQ, poor cognitive functioning and learning disabilities, and of exhibiting behavioural problems at school, even when parental social class and education are taken into account. Being born at a low weight therefore casts a long shadow over children's prospects of flourishing for the rest of their lives.

At the same time, large social inequalities exist in birth outcomes. Babies born to families on low incomes are significantly more likely to be born underweight than the population as a whole, with evidence also suggesting that factors such as parental unemployment, parental educational level and ethnicity are all significant contributors to low birth weight. Social inequalities in birth weight are an important factor in explaining other related inequalities, such as in infant mortality, where the rate among children in lower social classes is double that for higher social class groups.

One of the advantages of a life chances approach is that it necessitates an analysis of the range of factors that lead to bad outcomes for some groups of people. Maternal health and well being at the time of conception and through pregnancy are absolutely critical to the healthy development of the foetus. Maternal health and well being, in turn, are affected by a wide range of forces, from the individual behaviour and lifestyle choices of the mother, to her social and economic circumstances, her physical environment, the quality of her relations with others, and so on. One of the themes of this pamphlet – and an important premise of the life chances approach in general – is the complex causality underlying key outcomes, which are often determined by a whole set of interacting forces, both individual and societal.

Many of these forces, however, are susceptible to public policy interventions, which can therefore be used to narrow the gap in birth outcomes. As with government action in other policy areas, though, the motivation for, and legitimacy of, such interventions requires serious examination – particularly when focused on foetal development during pregnancy.

Motivating public policy interventions before birth

We believe that there are both strong moral and economic arguments for government action to improve life chances at birth. First of all, many of the arguments which are commonly made for investing in babies and children, and in sharing the costs associated with family life, are just as applicable to the period before birth as to later stages of development. For example, the economic case for intervention in the 'early years', which focuses on the potential benefits and savings for society of early investment, is based on the principle that intervening early is more productive and ultimately more cost-effective than responding to problems at the 'eleventh' hour, when it may be too late to avert an impending disaster.

This same logic can be extended to the 'pre-birth' period, as reducing the number of babies who are born too early or too small would arguably be more cost effective than the current reliance on high risk intensive care services for newborn babies. Over time, improvements in babies' birth outcomes would generate further savings by helping to reduce the long-term health, developmental and behavioural problems associated with very low birth weight, so reducing the ongoing medical and support service needs of these infants and their families, which add to the overall cost burden.[1]

Similarly, the moral case for government action to promote the life chances of children, especially those from low-income families, can also be extended to the 'pre-birth' period. This type of argument, as set out above, is made on the grounds of social justice. At its heart is the principle that every child should be given the chance to flourish, regardless of the circumstances of their birth. No one would pretend that differences in the social environment into which children are born could ever be completely eliminated. But there are strong moral grounds for wanting to give every child the best start in life, for example by redistributing resources from better off households to low-income families with children, or by taking action to improve babies' life chances at birth, by tackling the causes of poor birth outcomes. Unlike the economic arguments for intervention, the fundamental value here is intrinsic: even if such action did not offer any savings or benefits for society at large, it would still be morally right and justifiable to take action to improve a baby's life chances at birth.

There is an important distinction between the positive and negative case for intervention. A negative stance is not only more likely to generate a punitive narrative which focuses narrowly on individual behaviour and thereby apportions blame, it is also more likely to influence the character of policy implementation, particularly in the direction of attempts to constrain behaviour by imposing conditionality or sanctions. Though conditionality and sanctions may be legitimate aspects of welfare and service provision in certain contexts, in an area as sensitive as support during pregnancy, such an approach, as we discuss later, can be counterproductive. It can deter people from engaging with institutions that can improve outcomes.

A good example of some of the difficulties in framing the motivations behind this agenda can be seen by recalling media coverage of the Government's *Action Plan on Social Exclusion*, which was launched in September 2006. The *Action Plan* itself was a positive set of proposals, with plans for early identification and targeted support for the most vulnerable mothers and infants, beginning during pregnancy (through relatively 'soft' interventions, such as home visits for pregnant women from a trained nurse). Yet coverage of its pre-birth proposals were overshadowed by reports of 'baby asbos' and 'hard hitting measures' to prevent children from 'problem families' who pose a 'menace to society' from 'going off the rails'.[2] Though much of the media coverage was not a fair reflection of either the tone or content of the policy document itself, confusion about the nature of the proposals partly stemmed from some of the more negative language in which the proposals were presented in the publicity surrounding the launch, notably by the Prime Minister in a media interview in which he spoke of the need for early (including pre-birth) intervention to prevent 'children of dysfunctional families and teenage mothers' from 'going off the rails'.[3] The result was that what should have been welcomed as a positive contribution to improving life chances was attacked by some on the left, including Tony Benn, who described the idea of 'identifying troublesome children in the foetus' as 'eugenics, the sort of thing Hitler talked about'.[4]

As this episode illustrates, it matters how government action is framed, and whether a positive or negative case is made for pre-birth interventions. The economic case for intervention stresses the significant potential savings for society to be made from taking action early to prevent problems arising in the first place, rather than waiting until the 'crisis' point is reached later in life. But although some of these potential savings include the prospects of reducing criminality and anti-social behaviour, this is by no means the primary motivation or justification, and should not be presented as such.

Whenever Government is faced with poor outcomes amongst a particular social group (which may require measures targeted towards that group), there is a choice about the 'direction' and tone of its response. Rather than invoking negative reasons for intervening during pregnancy, we argue that a positive political narrative is needed, one which emphasises the progressive principles behind government action to improve babies' life chances at birth and to give every child the best possible start in life. After all, only by being clear about the positive progressive motivation behind such policy interventions can we ever gain more public support for the agenda of improving life chances for all.

10

“

2 | The facts about low birth weight

A baby's birth weight is the single most important factor in determining his or her survival and how well he or she will thrive. Maternity Alliance

This chapter sets out the key facts about low birth weight and birth outcomes in the UK, starting in the first section with a brief definition of the key terms and concepts. In the second section we go on to summarise the effects of low birth weight, setting out the consequences of poor birth outcomes for a baby's survival, healthy growth and development, and later life chances. In section three we focus on social inequalities in birth outcomes – on the class and ethnic gap in the weight and timing of birth, as well as variations by maternal age and marital status. Understanding the extent of these disparities in birth outcomes is so important, we argue, because monitoring inequalities over time not only helps to estimate overall service needs, but also to target interventions at those who are most in need of help and support by health professionals and maternity services.[1] Of course, to target interventions effectively, we need to know more than the incidence of low birth weight: we need to understand the factors which affect birth outcomes. Therefore, in the next chapter we go on to examine evidence about the main causes of low birth weight, identifying risk factors and protective factors, and explaining what this means for policy planning.

2.1 Defining low birth weight and restricted foetal growth

A baby's weight at birth (its birth weight) is an important indicator of its 'readiness' for birth, being closely linked to his or her prospects for survival in the critical first weeks of life, as well as to his or her chances of flourishing in childhood and in later life. Of the 698,556 live births in Britain in 2005, 53,789 (7.7 per cent) of these were born at a low birth weight. Babies born at a low birth weight (defined as less than 2,500 grams, or five and a half pounds) may have experienced an unusual rate of development, which often indicates complications with the pregnancy that may affect the baby or its mother.[2] Birth weight therefore tells us something important about the extent of foetal development, and whether the infant has experienced normal or restricted foetal growth.

A baby's weight at birth is closely related to the length of gestation (how many weeks the foetus develops in the womb during pregnancy).[3] Not surprisingly, babies born prematurely (under 37 weeks gestation) are more likely to be lighter than the average birth weight. However, premature babies will not necessarily be small for their gestational age: a baby who is born early may still be within the normal range of weight for that gestational age.[4,5]

While the majority of low birth weight infants (approximately two-thirds) are born prematurely, a significant minority (approximately one third) are born full term. In other words, some babies who are born early will not be underweight, while many babies who are born full term will be. More than 80 per cent of infants who are small for gestational age are born full term. Birth weight is arguably a better guide, therefore, to the infant's health and 'readiness' for birth, and so for this reason, we focus our attention in the analysis that follows on the problem of low birth weight rather than gestational age.

2.2 Effects of low birth weight and restricted foetal growth

The effects of low birth weight and restricted foetal growth can be severe. A baby born too small or too soon has a steeply inflated risk of developing neonatal complications, which at worst will lead to the baby's premature death. A baby's birth weight is therefore closely related to its prospects for survival in infancy: in 2004, two-thirds of all stillbirths and over 70 per cent of all neonatal deaths had a birth weight of less than 2500g, compared with only 7.6 per cent of all live births in England, Wales and elsewhere.[6]

As well as increasing an infant's risk of mortality, being born underweight casts a long shadow over a child's prospects of flourishing for the rest of his or her life. First of all, birth weight is a strong predictor of health outcomes in childhood and adulthood. Underweight babies who survive the precarious first months are still more likely to have disabilities, to be hospitalised, or to suffer brain damage. In later life, there is an increased chance of suffering chronic illnesses, such as diabetes, stroke and lung disease.[7] In addition, being born at a low birth weight increases an infant's chances of having developmental and behavioural problems, including poor language development, low IQ, poor cognitive functioning, and special educational needs,[8] as well as having long-term consequences for employment and earnings potential in adult life.[9]

Finally, it is important to emphasise the impact on families of having a baby born too small or too early. Whilst the experience of pregnancy and the first year of their child's life are generally stressful and challenging for most parents, parents of underweight babies face an additional set of challenges and sources of anxiety.[10] Coping with the worry and potential heartache of neonatal intensive care, for example, makes huge demands on parents' emotional resources, while the long-term developmental delays and impairment associated with very low birth weight can create a burden, both financially and on family relationships.[11]

2.3 Social inequalities in the incidence of low birth weight in the UK

Given the long term consequences of low birth weight, it is clearly a matter of concern that birth outcomes in the UK are actually worsening. Alongside an increase in the incidence of stillbirths, a rising number of babies in the UK are being born prematurely and at a low birth weight. Over the last twenty years, the proportion of low birth weight babies has risen from 6.7 per cent of births in 1989 to 7.6 per cent in 1999, to 7.8 per cent in 2006.[12] Worryingly, the risk of a baby being born at a low birth weight is greater in the United Kingdom than anywhere else in the European Union.

	birth weight	All births	
		N	%
	Total	645533	
	<1000	5469	0.8
Low	1000-1499	5369	0.8
	1500-1999	10234	1.7
	2000-2499	31495	4.9
	2500-2999	110046	17.1
Normal	3000-3499	228527	35.4
	3500-3999	181973	28.2
	4000+	71094	11.1

Figure 1: The distribution of all births according to birth weight, England and Wales, 2004

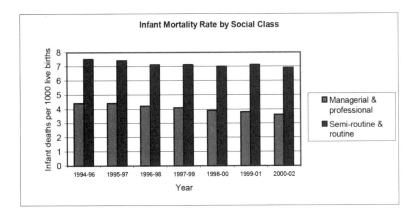

Figure 2: Infant mortality rate by social class
Source: ONS 2004.

Social inequalities in the incidence of low birth weight; Socio Economic Status (SES) and ethnicity

A clear social class divide exists in low birth weight: parents in routine manual occupations are 1.5 times more likely to have a low birth weight baby than parents in professional or managerial occupation.[13]

While the proportion of low birth weight babies rose steeply between 1993 and 2000, increasing by 10.8 per cent overall, increases were higher amongst manual (15.0 per cent) and sole registration groups (11.0 per cent) than in non-manual groups (8.8 per cent).[14]

The incidence of low birth weight also varies by ethnicity, with babies born to mothers of Indian, Pakistan and Bangladeshi origin being on average 300g lighter than their white counterparts.[15]

The class gap in infant and maternal mortality

The social class gap in the rate of low birth weight is an important factor in explaining the continued social inequalities in infant mortality.

As Figure 2 shows, the infant mortality rate among children in lower social classes was double that for higher social class groups in 2000-02, at 7.9 per cent compared to 3.6 per cent.

A social gradient in infant mortality exists across all classes: from four deaths per 1000 live births in social class I, to 5.4 in social class III (manual), 6.2 in social class IV and 8.1 in social class V.[16] The highest infant mortality rate during the period 1994 to 2002 was for babies registered by the mother alone (sole registration).

The incidence of low birth weight by maternal age

It is also relevant for our purposes that certain age groups of mothers are more likely to have a low birth weight baby than others. While younger and older mothers tend to have lighter babies, the group with the lowest proportion of low-weight babies in England and Wales, as well as the lowest rates of infant mortality, is that of mothers aged 30 to 34.[17]

Figures produced for this project by the Scottish Executive illustrate the size of the health gap between different age groups in Scotland. Between 2001 and 2005, the 30-34 age group had the lowest proportion of low-weight babies, 6.8 per cent, compared to 8.6 per cent and 8.5 per cent for the groups with the highest risk – mothers under twenty and over forty respectively (see Figure 3).

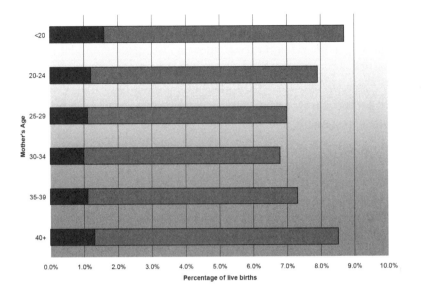

Figure 3: Percentage of live births (g) in Scotland by Mother's Age 2001-2005

Source: ISD Scotland SMR02/Ref IR2006-03224

2.4 Reasons for the rise in low birth weight: relevant social trends

Recent increases in the incidence of low birth weight need to be understood against the context of a number of social trends, including the rise of fertility treatment and multiple births (babies from multiple births tend to be smaller on average than singleton babies), and the enhanced survival rates of underweight babies, due to technical advances and improved neonatal care.[18]

Another contributory factor has been the general trend towards later childbearing, with a decline in birth rates for women in their 20s over the last forty years, and rising fertility rates for women in their 30s and early 40s. The number of pregnancies for women aged over 35 has risen dramatically in the last decade (increasing in England from 63,000 in 1993 to 103,000 in 2003), at the same time as the fertility rate for women aged 20-24 has fallen by almost half.[19]

Another relevant factor, and one which is important in explaining the higher incidence of low birth weight in the UK than in other European countries, is the high rate of teenage pregnancy in the UK.

These factors are discussed further in the next chapter, in which we examine the causes of low birth weight and, more importantly, the *causes* of the causes.

"

3 | Conceptualising the problem of low birth weight – and deciding the appropriate response

Research charting the effects of low birth weight helps build a compelling case for policy interventions to tackle the problem. But how should policy-makers respond?

Importantly, the nature of the policy response – including how 'hard' or 'soft' it should be, or how supportive or punitive – depends not only on what is being prevented, but how the health problem is conceptualised. In particular, it matters how social inequalities in health are presented, as different policy responses are called for if the problem is conceived as resulting primarily from the effects of 'risky' and health damaging behaviours, such as smoking or eating unhealthily, than if there is recognition of the underlying socio-economic factors too.[1] With this in mind this section explores how to think about the causes of low birth weight.

3.1 Understanding the causes of low birth weight

As outlined in section 2.1, low birth weight is caused either by a short gestation period or by restricted foetal growth, or a combination of both. The direct or immediate causes of restricted foetal growth can be separated into a number of main categories, including maternal health, placental, and foetal factors (see Box 2). [2]

Box 2: The immediate causes of low birth weight: restricted foetal growth and preterm birth

Restricted foetal growth has mixed causal pathways and more than one etiological factor may be responsible in any given case. The main causes can be summarised as follows:

- maternal health factors, including malnutrition, severe anaemia, excessive energy consumption, addictions (alcohol, smoking, drugs), chronic respiratory diseases, heart diseases, pregnancy-induced hypertension;
- placental factors such as chronic placental separation and utero-placental insufficiency;
- and foetal factors, including structural anomalies such as congenital heart disease, collagen and musculo-skeletal disorders, or foetal infections, e.g. viral infections such as rubella, listeriosis, tuberculosis.

Preterm birth results from one or more causal processes – for example, because the mother has contracted an infection, or because the growth of the foetus has been restricted (perhaps due to nutritional defects during pregnancy) – which may operate separately or interact with one another. In practice, the causes of prematurity and foetal growth restriction frequently interact.

As Box 2 indicates, the causes of low birth weight are multiple and overlapping, and the precise cause(s) is often difficult to diagnose (which can create problems for treating the condition, as we explore further in Chapter 6). However, by analysing 'risk' factors we are able to identify a number of elements that clearly increase the probability of low birth weight. We know, for example, that infants whose mothers smoke during pregnancy have a lower birth weight on average (typically 150 to 200 grams less) than children of non-smokers (controlling for other parental background factors, such as income and education).[3] A recent r cause of low birth weight and a key risk factor for stillbirth, neonatal death and SIDS (Sudden Infant Death Syndrome or cot death)."[4] There is also very clear evidence of the links between low birth weight and maternal diet and nutrition. Repeated studies have shown that low birth weight is influenced by a number of nutritional factors, including pre-pregnancy maternal weight, gestational weight gain, energy intake, iron and anaemia.[5]

Importantly, we also know that women from lower income and SES backgrounds are more likely to smoke and less likely to have access to an adequate diet than other women: While 20 per cent of all mothers smoke during pregnancy, 29 per cent of women in manual occupations and 36 per cent of women who had never worked were smokers in 2000, compared to 8 per cent of women in managerial and professional occupations.[6] This is despite the fact that the vast majority of pregnant women can recall being given advice regarding the health risks of smoking during pregnancy.

Research into low birth weight also reveals a social class gradient in maternal nutritional status, with women on low incomes – and teenagers in particular – more likely than other women to consume no fruit or vegetables on a typical day, to miss meals, and to be deficient in essential vitamins, minerals and proteins.[7]

The trouble with laying out the bare facts in this way is that it has the potential to feed into a widespread tendency to 'individualise' responsibility for foetal well-being and place this responsibility solely on the mother.[8] This approach, which is evidenced in traditional conservative narratives about maternal responsibility, tends to focus exclusively on maternal risk behaviours, particularly instances of maternal-foetal conflict (where there is an apparent trade-off in well-being between the two).

Such a narrow view clearly ignores a wide range of factors that affect foetal development, by acting both on the foetus directly and also on the mother. Environmental toxins and other factors (such as disease, damp or noise) to which the pregnant woman can be exposed, can obviously affect both her health and that of the foetus. Other types of external factors can have more subtle and multi-faceted effects on maternal and foetal health. Emotional abuse can lead to stress and anxiety that have both direct biological effects and in turn can drive maternal behaviour, such as smoking. Physical abuse can obviously damage both maternal and foetal health directly, as well as affecting maternal behaviour more widely. Financial hardship can directly constrain factors like maternal diet, as well as generating stress that can affect other maternal behaviour.

Furthermore, over the last two decades, a body of evidence has been accumulating linking male reproductive health with birth outcomes such as miscarriage, low birth weight and congenital abnormalities. Studies have shown associations between foetal health problems and particular occupational exposures to toxic substances (e.g. toluene, benzene, lead, mercury, etc.), as well as with exposures resulting from 'lifestyle factors' such as paternal smoking – though the trend of individualising responsibility has also ensured that research showing the links between male reproductive health and adverse birth outcomes has not received the same media attention as those relating to pregnant women's behaviour.[9]

Foetal development is thus seen as affected by a complex and interrelated set of forces acting both on the foetus directly and also on the mother. This analysis – as illustrated in the diagrams below – therefore represents a 'widening out' of the picture of factors affecting foetal development – from the narrow view focussed on solely on maternal decisions and actions, to one which also encompasses a range of factors affecting the pregnant woman herself, including those that shape her decisions and actions.

Figure 4: A narrow view of factors affecting foetal development

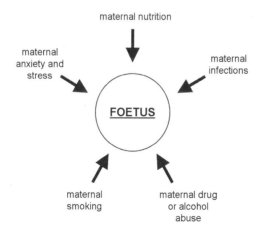

21

Figure 5: A wider view of factors affecting foetal development

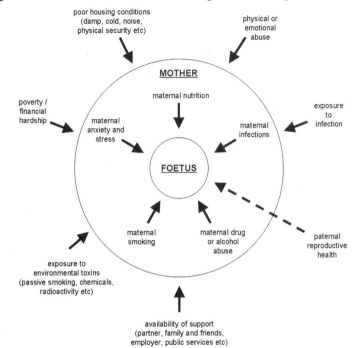

Without undermining notions of maternal responsibility, this analysis recognises the potential contributions of a range of actors – individual, social and institutional – to foetal well-being:

- **Mother** gestational contribution, with unique responsibilities.
- **Father** – potential provision of support; potential exposure to smoke or disease; potential physical abuse or contribution to maternal stress; (in the case of the biological father) potential production of damaged sperm, etc.
- **Family, friends and colleagues** – potential provision of support; potential exposure to smoke or disease, etc.
- **Employer** – potential to accommodate the pregnant woman's workplace needs; potential contribution to maternal stress;

potential exposure to occupational hazards and toxins, etc.
- **Government** – potential to provide of financial support, health services, adequate housing; potential to regulate of exposure to hazardous substances, etc.

In doing so, we move away from an approach which focuses responsibility solely on the pregnant woman. Furthermore, it can require us to focus on the mother and foetus as a single unit on which external forces act, meaning a concern for the well-being of the foetus must be reflected in a duty of care to the pregnant woman.

3.2 Understanding the *causes* of the causes

If we want both to understand the causes of low birth weight, and to devise ways of responding to the problem, we need to understand the underlying background factors which shape health behaviours. In particular, we need to ask why women from lower income and lower status groups are much more likely than other women to smoke or to be nutritionally vulnerable. What, in other words, are the *causes* of the causes: what is it about living on a very low income that makes it more likely that someone will engage in 'risky' health behaviours, such as smoking, that may be detrimental to foetal development and infant health?

One possible explanation is that people from lower income and lower SES groups simply have a less informed view about what constitutes a healthy diet or healthy lifestyle. Certainly, lack of knowledge or information may be a factor in some cases, but it is not the sole or even the main barrier, as can be seen by the fact that nutritional interventions to promote healthy eating, have been shown to be effective in increasing nutritional knowledge without having any impact on dietary intake. It follows that there are other barriers or obstacles associated with living in disadvantaged circumstances, or on a very low income, which impact on a woman's health, and the health of her children (including those as yet unborn).

To understand the health gap, we need to understand how features of women's social circumstances and environment have an impact on behaviours that may contribute to poor health.[10] In the case of poor diet, people living on very low incomes face material obstacles to attaining a balanced, nutritious diet, not least of which is the cost of buying healthy ingredients (and also basic cooking equipment), but also lack of access to shops selling healthy food – something which is particularly difficult for people living in areas which are not well-serviced by local shops ('food deserts'), and for the one in six households who do not own a car to drive to cheaper outlets sited away from residential areas. Disadvantaged women therefore "often face greater barriers to choosing a healthier personal lifestyle because of lack of income, time or opportunity".[11]

Research has provided some insight as to why people on lower incomes and in lower status jobs are more likely to indulge in health threatening behaviours, even when they are pregnant. An important part of the explanation for the class gap in smoking, meanwhile, lies in the pressures experienced by people on low incomes. For many low income women, smoking provides an outlet for the release of anxiety or tension, despite its known health risks.[12] There is also evidence that people who live and grow up in disadvantaged circumstances tend to have more fatalistic attitudes towards their health, and are more likely to view health outcomes as something that is impossible to control or change. It may thus be the case that disadvantaged young people are less likely to heed anti-smoking health warnings because they feel no control over their lives, and see little point in struggling to give up smoking for the sake of their health.[13]

None of the preceding discussion about the underlying causes of maternal and infant ill-health means that we should be any less assiduous in working to reduce smoking and alcohol use during pregnancy, in promoting access to a healthy diet amongst disadvantaged groups, particularly young women living on low incomes, and in reducing inequalities in access to health services. But the complexity of these causal relations should give cause to reflect on conventional media narratives about maternal responsibility and simplistic moral evaluations of maternal behaviour.

Understanding these kinds of pressures should not only provide a more sophisticated basis for evaluating and judging behaviour, but will be crucial to finding the appropriate public policy interventions to respond to the problem of low birth weight.

The links between low income and low birth weight

Living on a low income or in deprived circumstances has a direct impact on health: for example, by limiting the affordability of healthy food, or because substandard accommodation and a poor quality physical environment leads to respiratory problems and infectious diseases. But it also has indirect effects, because having to make ends meet on a very low income increases the risk of stress and mental ill-health, which are themselves associated with poor pregnancy outcomes. As recent research has revealed, maternal stress during pregnancy is linked both to reduced uterine blood flow (which leads to retarded growth in the uterus) and to higher cortisol levels for mother and baby.

The experience of poverty and deprivation can therefore trigger biological stress responses, which are then passed on to babies before they are born. As well as increasing the risk of restricted foetal growth, the higher cortisal levels which are passed on to babies are linked to higher rates of disease in later life.[14] Maternal stress and anxiety during pregnancy also increases the chances that children will develop emotional and behavioural problems in early childhood.[15] Thus, along with maternal nutrition and smoking during pregnancy, maternal stress during pregnancy is a major risk factor associated with low birth weight, which affects babies' health and developmental outcomes even before birth.

Poverty and material deprivation can also impact on maternal and infant health by negatively affecting women's access to or use of antenatal services and maternity care. The 'inverse care law' in health care – by which medical care is least available where it is most needed – is widely recognised today.[16] In the case of antenatal care, the actual evidence of social class differences in access is somewhat conflicting: NPEU's systematic review of the evidence concluded that there have been "few recent reviews or studies of the extent to which social factors influence the use of health care".[17] More recently, however, data provided by the Millennium Cohort Study has produced evidence to confirm sizeable variation between ethnic groups in attendance at antenatal classes, which are correlated with a longer gestation period and a higher birth weight for babies.

Attendance at antenatal classes is lower for ethnic minority mothers than for white mothers, though attendance for all groups is still very low: 22 per cent of mothers of Asian children, 29 per cent of mothers of Black children and 33 per cent of mothers of children of mixed or other ethnic origins attend antenatal classes, compared with 40 per cent of mothers of White children.[18] For non-white women, a lower level of access to care, including late booking (>22 weeks) and poor or no antenatal clinic attendance, is identified as a key factor explaining the greater risk they face of maternal death during child-birth as compared to white women.[19] Problems of accessing proper maternity care are particularly acute for non-English speaking women or those with little language fluency, who may experience difficulties communicating with health practitioners without effective language support from independent interpreters. In addition, there is strong evidence that pregnant teenagers are less likely to use ante-natal services, and more likely to report problems developing a good relationship with health practitioners than other age-groups.[20]

The links between socio-demographic factors and low birth weight

The complexity of these causal relations can be further illustrated by looking at other risk factors for low birth weight, namely maternal age and family structure. In the case of teenage mothers, we know that younger mothers are much more likely, on average, than other mothers to have a birth outside marriage and to register the birth on their own, as well as being more likely to come from disadvantaged backgrounds and to have poor educational attainment.[21] However, while early moth-erhood it is a risk factor for a whole set of disadvantages, including low birth weight, it does not follow that it is the *cause* of the problem.[22] In fact, analysis of Census data shows that the increased risk of low birth weight for these mothers is entirely accounted for by their deprived socio-economic circumstances.[23]

In other words, age is not the determining factor here, but rather a function of the fact that women who have a baby at a young age are far more likely to come from disadvantaged backgrounds than other mothers. Relatedly, while the later negative effects associated with early motherhood are well documented, it does not mean that the relationship is necessarily causal: rather than early motherhood being the cause of future disadvantage, it is possible that this reflects prior disadvantage. Whereas policies to reduce the teenage conception rate are premised on the assumption that early motherhood causes later disadvantage, these policies will be less effective if early motherhood actually reflects prior disadvantage. If this is the case, interventions need to start much earlier, to address the socio-economic circumstances which both increase the likelihood of early motherhood and are the cause of later negative outcomes.[24] These issues are discussed further in Chapter 7, when we consider the appropriate policy response to the high incidence of low birth weight amongst teenage mothers.

Turning to another socio-demographic factor, what explains the strong relationship between a baby's birth weight and family structure, or parents' marital or relationship status? As with teenage parents, the fact that solely registered births have a higher risk of low birth weight than other births does not mean that mother's marital or relationship status is the causal factor. We know, for example, that lone mothers are generally younger and more disadvantaged, on average, than mothers who are married or cohabiting with their partners.[25] Lone mothers are also more likely to be unemployed, on low income, to have no educational qualifications and to have no car.[26] For lone mothers, as for younger mothers, therefore, the high incidence of low birth weight is very strongly connected to their adverse socio-economic circumstances. However, unlike teenage mothers, lone parents' higher risk of low birth weight cannot entirely be explained by socio-economic factors: the risks appear to persist even when the substantial effect of increased poverty and deprivation levels in lone parent families have been taken into account.[27] This raises the interesting question of whether additional policy responses to the problem of low birth weight are needed in the case of lone mothers.

Interestingly, a rather different picture emerges for 'older' mothers, whose socio-demographic profile is strikingly different. Women who have babies in their late thirties and forties are much more likely to be university graduates and to be working in managerial or professional occupations than younger mothers: new mothers aged 35 and above are twice as likely to be in managerial and professional jobs as new mothers aged 25 to 29 and four times as likely as new mothers aged 20 to 24.[28] Women in their thirties and above are also more likely to be in a relationship when they start a family than younger mothers,[29] which may help explain the fact that 'older' women's pregnancies are more likely to have been planned.[30]

Of course, later parenthood is not just a trend amongst the well off: of the 2904 babies born to women aged 35 and over in the Millennium Cohort Study (out of a total of 18503 births), approximately one quarter were born to women in 'routine and manual' occupations or no stated occupation, one quarter to women in 'intermediate' occupations, and just under fifty per cent were born to women in managerial and professional occupations (47.3 per cent).[31] Nevertheless, the striking differences in the socio-demographic profiles of older mothers indicate that a different set of causal processes are operating than for teenage mothers.

Part of the explanation for the higher rate of low birth weight amongst women in their forties lies in their higher incidence of multiple births. Not only is the proportion of multiple births rising due to increased use of assisted reproductive technologies, it is also the case that older mothers are more likely to conceive multiple pregnancies naturally than younger mothers. However, although the increase in multiple births is a contributing factor to the increase in low birth weight rates, low birth weight has also increased among singleton deliveries for older mothers. The reasons for this appear to lie in the higher incidence of placental problems and foetal infections amongst older mothers.

However, while the biological mechanisms are different in the case of the typical 'younger' and 'older' mother, in both cases it is important to recognise the multiplicity of factors which impact on the mother and baby, many of which are outside the control of the individuals concerned. As with other 'high risk' groups or categories of pregnant women, we need to reject an 'individualist' approach which assumes that women are isolated units making independent choices about when to start a family. In particular, we need to take into account the range of social changes which have contributed to the trend towards later child-bearing in the last twenty to thirty years (these will be explored in Chapter 7). As different causal processes are operating in the case of teenage and older parents, the appropriate policy response in each case will differ accordingly.

3.3 Determining the appropriate policy response

There are a number of different types of policy response that we could make to address the range of factors that contribute to low birth weight. They will differ in terms of when they occur in the pre-birth period, and who they are designed to target.

For example, as represented in Figure 6, some forms of intervention

Nature of intervention	Timing of intervention		
	Pre-conception	Early Stages	Later stages
Universal	(1)	(2)	(3)
Targeted	(4)	(5)	(6)

Figure 6: Matrix of policy interventions

will be apply to all women of child-bearing age prior to conception, such as general health and fertility advice (1); while routine antenatal services available to all pregnant women would fall under (2) and (3). An example of (4) would be a strategy targeting groups at particularly high risk of poor pregnancy outcomes prior to conception, such as the Teenage Pregnancy Strategy; while (5) and (6) could apply to specific measures taken to diagnose and monitor restricted foetal growth for 'at risk' groups, as well as targeted support services (such as the kinds of special support outlined in the *Action Plan on Social Exclusion*).

The nature of the policy response will also vary in terms of how intrusive it is, in both a clinical and social sense. Decisions about how appropriate intrusive medical interventions are will largely be made on the grounds of medical need. However, in deciding how appropriate a potentially socially intrusive policy will be, policy makers will need to assess the political and moral case for that policy, along with the precedence.

We have identified two principles to help us formulate an appropriate policy response, which are informed by our previous analysis:

Prevention is better than cure:
Preventing the problem arising in the first place is more humane, as well as being more cost effective, than treatment of the condition once it has arisen. While it is absolutely essential to ensure sufficient resources to allow clinicians to monitor and treat foetal infections or restricted foetal growth – relying on provision of 'high risk' intensive care is ultimately more costly, for babies, families and society, than preventing the problem arising in the first place.

Preventing the problem depends on understanding the deeper underlying causes:
We recognise that the causes of low birth weight are multiple, complex and overlapping. Analysis of 'risk factors' helps us identify a number of immediate causes, including a number of

'negative' health behaviours. But underpinning the immediate causes is a wider set of background factors – including
structural or socio-economic factors such as inequalities in
income, status and education, which need to be taken into
account. So, while recognising the unique nature of maternal
responsibility for foetal well being, we need to avoid simply
individualising responsibility through a narrow focus on
maternal behaviour.

95046

‟

4 | Providing the best start in life for the most vulnerable infants

So how should policy-makers respond to the problem of low birth weight? As with the Government's Teenage Pregnancy Strategy, which is founded on the twin principles of prevention and providing adequate support, a two-fold strategy is needed to prevent and manage the problem of low birth weight. In this chapter we look at the provision of support for those who are born with a low birth weight, and suggest improvements to antenatal and neonatal services designed to minimise the negative impact of low birth weight in the period immediately after birth. In the subsequent chapters we focus on investment in preventing the problem arising in the first place.

Importantly, as well as discussing the efficacy of policies focused on specific causes of ill-health, primarily poor diet and smoking, which we examine in Chapter 5, in Chapter 6 we go on to consider what types of interventions are needed to address the underlying socio-economic factors, which lie at the heart of social inequalities in birth outcomes. In particular, we focus on the types of financial support that are needed during pregnancy and also prior to conception, to ease pressures on families and help provide women with a nutritionally adequate diet.

Finally, in Chapter 7, we ask what the appropriate political and policy response should be to a different background factor, namely maternal age. We argue that although there is good evidence linking certain socio-demographic trends with the rising incidence of low birth weight, it does not necessarily follow that an explicit 'population policy' is needed in response. Rather, the Government should continue to pursue 'family-friendly' policies, such as flexible working arrangements, which can have an indirect effect on trends such as maternal age at pregnancy, as well as considering the implications for related areas of policy such as higher education, and as employment patterns over the life course.

4.1 Monitoring and treatment of the baby's growth during pregnancy

During pregnancy, the growth of the foetus will need to be kept under close review to ensure early and reliable diagnosis, starting with accurate dating of the pregnancy (through detailed menstrual history and first trimester or early second trimester USG scan) and a detailed family history to be aware of parental health factors associated with low birth weight. Close antenatal monitoring is needed during the second and third trimesters, particularly for those pregnant women with a higher than average risk of having a low birth weight baby, to create a meticulous record of maternal weight gain and to detect any evidence of foetal growth lagging as early as possible.[1]

As restricted foetal growth is associated with a fivefold increase in the stillbirth rate, and a threefold increase in neonatal mortality, the later stages of pregnancy and labour will need to be closely monitored. In the most severe cases, difficult decisions will need to be taken about the optimum timing and mode of delivery, as the risks of gross prematurity will need to be weighed against the risks of a severely growth-restricted foetus suffering from intra uterine foetal demise. Short term and long term follow-up of these babies is essential, because of their increased risk of suffering complications such as hypertension, dyslipidaemia and coronary heart disease in their future life.

In policy terms, the goal for antenatal management of low birth weight is therefore to ensure that resources are available to monitor and treat those women who are most at risk of experiencing problems during pregnancy. Perhaps the biggest challenge here is to address social inequalities in maternity care, to ensure that every woman whose baby is at risk of restricted foetal growth is able to access antenatal services. Women on low incomes face a range of barriers to accessing maternity care, including transport difficulties, long inflexible working hours or caring duties, while the most vulnerable pregnant women may be reluctant to meet with health practitioners or to attend antenatal clinics because of language difficulties or perceptions that they will be judged negatively.[2] Adequate resources are needed, therefore, to provide specialist training for nurses and health practitioners who work with the most vulnerable groups of pregnant women, such as young mothers and asylum seekers. These extra resources could be found through increased investment in maternity care, or by rebalancing maternity services to release resources for outreach work to reach the most vulnerable groups.

Recommendation 1: Reduce social inequalities in access to maternity care

More needs to be done to reduce social inequalities in access to maternity care, especially through investing in specially trained nursing staff and outreach workers to help meet the needs of pregnant women most at risk of having a sick, premature or underweight baby. This extra investment could be achieved either through an increase in overall funding for maternity care, or by rebalancing antenatal services: as the UK currently aims for a relatively high number of antenatal appointments for pregnant women – 13 compared to 9 in many EU countries – the standard number of antenatal visits could be reduced without negatively affecting maternal or infant health, which would then release additional resources to focus support on the most disadvantaged groups of pregnant women.

Recent local campaigns against the reconfiguration of maternity services are a reminder of how contentious this kind of 'rebalancing' can be – especially when the motivation for change is perceived as being financial or political, rather than driven by the best clinical practice. So it is important to be clear about the rationale behind any such proposal, to reassure women that changes to the existing pattern of care are consistent with best practice and will not compromise the care of themselves and their babies.

The provision of NHS maternity services is moving towards a maternity network model, which aims to give pregnant women the choice of a range of settings in which to give birth, consisting of: hospital-based care by a local maternity team including a consultant obstetrician (linked to neonatal intensive care units); midwife-led maternity units, attached either to hospitals or in community settings, and home births supported by experienced midwife.

For women and babies requiring longer and more complex care, the development of maternity networks should enable the concentration of clinical skills and expertise, to ensure the best standards of maternity and neonatal care. But while the concentration of clinical expertise in fewer specialised care units should allow for the best use to be made of obstetricians and obstetric anaesthetists, the major concern is about whether adequate staffing levels, particularly of specially trained nurses and midwives, will be achieved.[3] Ideally, the reorganisation of maternity services would have happened at the same time as the development of neonatal networks, as the upheaval generated by the changes creates a background of uncertainty for staff working in the service.

Setting out the clinical case for the changes, the National Clinical Director for Children, Young people and Maternity Services, Sheila Shribman, has argued that the reorganisation will release resources to provide more community midwives to help meet the particular needs of the most vulnerable pregnant women.[4] This type of community based work, in which midwives work alongside community workers and interpreters, Sure Start Children's Centres, social services and GPs, is crucial to help reach the most vulnerable women, particularly the significant minority (30 per cent) of the lowest-income women who do not contact their maternity services until they are at least five months pregnant.[5]

As well as increasing choice of birth settings, therefore, the development of maternity networks has the potential to improve the life chances of women and babies, particularly the groups most at risk of low birth weight and other poor birth outcomes. On these grounds, the development of maternity networks is to be welcomed, providing that sufficient resources are available to guarantee the necessary staffing levels to achieve the best standards of care.

4.2 Neonatal services for the most vulnerable newborn babies

Whilst prevention may be better than cure, it is vital to have in place policies which minimise the negative impact of being born with a low birth weight. For infants born with very low birth weights, their chances of surviving this critical period, and of flourishing for the rest of their lives, will depend on the quality of neonatal care they receive. Specialist and intensive care must be made available for all babies who need it in the vulnerable period immediately after birth. Adequate resources are essential to enable clinicians and health professionals to offer comprehensive advice and care to pregnant women and their partners, and to provide specialist support for babies who are born at a low birth weight.

For those low birth weight babies that need to spend time in a neonatal unit, it is essential that the resources are available to provide the optimum level of neonatal care. Yet at present, there is a worrying shortage of specialist (Level 3) units, which provide intensive care for the smallest and most dependent babies.[6] Recent research reveals that almost 90% of intensive care units in 2006 had to close to new admissions in the last six months.[7] The very high incidence of specialist units becoming full up is a cause for serious concern, because it means that the smallest and most vulnerable babies and mothers are either transferred to another specialist unit, which may well be some distance away, or they are cared for in a Level 1 or 2 neonatal unit, which lacks the expertise of the specialist unit.[8]

The necessary funding, therefore, needs to be available to ensure that every sick, premature or underweight baby has access to the appropriate level of care. Provision needs to be made for staffed costs at different levels (intensive, high dependency or special care) to avoid babies being transferred away from the local area due to shortages of appropriate care.[9] Importantly, analysis shows that what is needed is not so much an increase in the number of staffed cots in intensive care units, but better clinical management of units, to prevent 'bed blocking' in intensive care. This occurs when babies needing high dependency and special care are placed in intensive care units, which then denies places to sicker or more dependent babies.[10]

The biggest need in neonatal care is an increase of nursing staff. National surveys of the capacity and organisation of neonatal units in the UK, conducted by Oxford University's National Perinatal Institute (NPEU), reveal a marked shortfall in the recommended staffing levels for nurses: of 143 surveyed units, only 3 achieved the recommended nursing level in 2006. Shortfalls also exist in the number of specially trained nurses in neonatal care units: although the proportion of nurses with a specialist qualification increased by 10 per cent in the past ten years to 63 per cent, this still falls short of the recommended level of 70 per cent.[11]

To achieve the optimum level of care for the most vulnerable infants neonatal services need to offer the same levels of staffing for babies in intensive care as is already the norm for adult patients. Although the need for one to one nursing for babies in intensive care was acknowledged in the Government's 2003 review of neonatal services, the Department of Health has yet to make it mandatory.

Planned changes to NHS funding could also be used to encourage investment in nursing staff, when neonatal intensive care is incorporated into the Payment By Results (PBR) system in April 2008, (whereby hospital trusts will be paid for each activity they perform, rather than in block budgets).

Rather than being based on average funding at present levels (which as we have seen is currently inadequate to meet staffing levels), the PBR tariff could be set above average funding, and should include a 'specialist top-up'. This would allow neonatal units to invest in nursing staff and so reach the standard of one nurse looking after one baby in intensive care. However, neonatal networks need to explore ways of promoting staff retention.

This level of staffing care would help meet the wider needs of parents, whose relationship with neonatal staff is so important in helping them cope with their baby's condition.[12] Parents need to have access to emotional and relationship support at this difficult and stressful time, as well as help and assistance in practical ways, for example in accessing financial support.[13] Helping parents cope with the stressful experience of having a baby in neonatal care is particularly important, because parental anxiety due to hospitalisation in the first weeks of life has been identified as a causal factor in later behavioural problems associated with being born early, such as temper tantrums and emotional problems.[14] Medical and health practitioners such as midwives and health visitors have an essential bridging role to play, helping to build and sustain relationships with parents, especially the most vulnerable or disadvantaged, who may benefit most from information and advice about how to avoid the problem of low birth weight in subsequent pregnancies. The ability of neonatal services to fulfil this role will also depend on staffing levels, and the availability of specially trained staff to undertake this type of guidance and advice.

Recommendation 2: One-to-one nursing care for the most vulnerable infants

Although the most vulnerable infants – those born sick, premature and underweight – ought to be entitled to the optimum level of neonatal care, marked shortfalls remain in nursing staff levels and in the number of specially trained nurses in neonatal care units. The Department of Health has acknowledged the need for one to one nursing for babies in neonatal intensive care (as is already the norm for adult patients in intensive care). But it has yet to make this standard of care mandatory, and so must do so as an urgent priority. To promote staff recruitment and retention, neonatal units should be encouraged to adopt more flexible ways of working and incentivised to invest in training more nurses with specialist expertise.

"

5 | Preventative strategies: improving maternal and infant health

5.1 Changing health behaviours: the efficacy of policy interventions

There is an urgent need to address the two leading causes of low birth weight, smoking and poor diet, both during pregnancy and prior to conception.

One approach for policy-makers is to try to identify effective ways of changing health behaviours, particularly amongst the groups most at risk of smoking and poor diet. At the 'softer' end of the spectrum, the Government has a relatively uncontroversial role to play in the provision of public information and advice.[1] As well as providing information for the general public, the Department of Health supports the work of general medical practitioners, nurses and other health professionals, by providing materials and guidance, information to be given to patients, and practical advice on how to communicate public health messages to patients.[2]

The success of these 'softer' forms of government action clearly depends on the effectiveness of practitioners in communicating public health messages and the readiness of patients and members of the public to respond to that information. Evidence that public health messages, for example on the health risks associated with smoking, have been effective can be seen in the fact that patterns of smoking behaviour have altered significantly over the last forty years, as public information and awareness of the health risks has grown. But we also know that middle income, higher income and higher educated groups are more likely, on average, to respond to health messages than lower income and lower educated groups. The dilemma here is that universal or 'primary' prevention strategies, such as public health campaigns aimed at the general population, are likely to be differentially effective, and may even have the effect of widening health gaps, because people from different income or social groups respond differently to those health messages.

In attempting to narrow the gaps in health outcomes and health behaviour: a range of strategies will be needed to ensure that the message actually gets through, and that it reaches those who do not heed the advice communicated through general public health announcements. Thus, alongside universal public health provision and general public health campaigns, any effective strategy to narrow health inequalities must include targeted measures aimed at changing the behaviour of specific groups.

Part of the difficulty here is that despite strong evidence on the links between birth outcomes and the relevant risk factors, the evidence of what works to improve birth outcomes is much less robust. In the case of healthy eating during pregnancy, for example, we know that "it is easier to improve a woman's nutritional knowledge (for example, through nutrition classes or leaflets) than to affect her dietary intake". [3]

This lack of evidence of 'what works' highlights a number of methodological problems which urgently need to be addressed. In the first place, a greater commitment is needed to build up a body of knowledge through the replication of research findings in subsequent studies, to encourage larger sample sizes and to fund the kinds of randomised control trials which are the 'gold standard' for evaluation studies. A further problem relates to the difficulties of rolling out interventions which have been shown to be effective in particular locations: after all, it is not enough to demonstrate the efficacy of a particular programme or intervention for participants; further research is often needed to find out whether positive outcomes can be replicated for other types of participants or in different settings.[4] Adequate funding therefore needs to be available in order to conduct high quality research, including the 'gold standard' of randomised control trials, and in order to replicate these findings in multiple settings.

Crucially, however, lack of evidence about 'what works' should not be taken as evidence that nothing works – rather, we should see it as a sign of lack of investment in investigations and evaluations to establish what strategies are effective.[5]

Recommendation 3: Make reducing low birth weight a national health and social priority

> *The Government must signal its determination to improve birth outcomes by making a reduction in low birth weight a national health and social priority. As part of this, a greater commitment is needed at the national level to address the paucity of knowledge about what kinds of policies can be effective in promoting maternal and infant health. To build up the evidence base on effective policy interventions, Government must demonstrate this commitment by increasing investment in rigorous research studies (for example, to encourage larger sample sizes and to fund randomised control trials).*

The legitimacy of 'harder' forms of intervention

More difficult questions about the role of the state arise when 'softer' and more neutral forms of intervention do not prove to be effective – that is, when people do not act voluntarily to change their health behaviour. In such cases, there may be grounds for 'harder', potentially more intrusive forms of government action, such as making entitlement to benefits dependent upon compliance with a set of health-related requirements. But what are the grounds for these 'harder' interventions, and what impact might they have?

The use of harder sanctions and condition can be contentious. For example, anti-poverty campaigners object to the element of conditionality introduced by the Government's Healthy Start scheme whereby pregnant women and new mothers on income support are only eligible for vouchers for milk, fruit and vegetables, providing they first register for the programme with a health professional, who is then required to impart health advice and information.[6]

In principle, we might even say that the imposition of conditions in this way was justifiable if it improved pregnancy and birth outcomes for the most vulnerable women and infants. But while the requirement to register may be well-intended, there are concerns in practice that it has reduced or delayed take-up because some pregnant women are deterred from applying.[7] Critics are also concerned that it has had a detrimental impact on the nature of the relationship between the health professional and their clients.

There is, moreover, something objectionable about the trend towards increasing conditionality in the benefits available for *low*-income groups. According to Kate Green, chief executive of the Child Poverty Action Group, because there is no equivalent income sanction for those not reliant on state support, "policies to support progressive universalism and responsibilities coupled with rights have proved in practice to be discriminatory, discretionary and judgmental".[8]

The use of conditionality in this case therefore raises wider questions about the sensitivity of the devices or 'levers' that Government can pull to effect changes in health behaviour, and the justifiability of attempting to use rather crude or heavy handed measures to bring about behavioural change. Although there are good reasons for wanting to concentrate resources on the most disadvantaged groups of people, the worry is that the increased use of 'targeted' services will have the counter-productive effect of stigmatising those individuals, thereby exacerbating problems of take-up, by making people more reluctant to make use of services which are nominally available to them.

In some quarters, anxiety about the ramifications of 'harder' or more punitive forms of intervention have generated concerns about whether Government should legitimately be involved in 'pre-birth' interventions at all. In light of these concerns, it is worth briefly examining the principle of targeted intervention, to ask whether they are justified in the pre-birth period.

5.2 Coordinated and intensive support for the most vulnerable groups

Targeting at risk groups, rather than the occurrence of individual problems, can be an effective strategy because of the extent to which problems overlap, as "preventative programmes, whether targeting individuals or whole communities, are more likely to be effective when they are designed to reduce multiple risks".[9] For example, evidence from the Avon study shows that people on low income are more likely to smoke and to have dietary deficiencies. Rather than focusing on any single nutritional supplement or smoking cessation strategy, we need preventative strategies which treat people holistically. Thus, instead of asking what kinds of behaviour needs to be targeted, we should ask which groups of people are most at risk of that kind of behaviour, and how best can they be helped to achieve better health?

It is important to recognise here that the most vulnerable and most disadvantaged individuals – the 'hardest to reach' – often have complex needs that may span a range of health and social issues, from mental health problems and substance abuse, to living in a deprived area and lack of access to safe, decent housing. Crucially, the range of problems affecting any individual will vary from person to person, which therefore requires a tailored or personalised response from public and social services.[10]

The principle of early identification

In the case of low birth weight, the kinds of coordinated support which are needed to help improve the pregnancy outcomes of the most vulnerable pregnant women, will need to begin very early: certainly before birth, and possibly even prior to conception. It is this insight which informs the principle of 'early identification and early intervention', which is a cornerstone of the recent *Action Plan on Social Exclusion*.[11]   Drawing on research evidence collected by behavioural and developmental psychologists led by Carole Sutton, Vivette Glover and colleagues, the *Action Plan* highlights the role of midwives and health visitors in identifying at-risk groups during pregnancy and building up strong relationships with families from the start. The *Action Plan* also sets out a commitment to conduct 10 pilot studies to build up precisely the kind of research evidence that is needed to demonstrate the efficacy of early interventions.

Though we have reservations about framing the *Action Plan* around anti-social behaviour, the Government's commitment to this kind of intervention is very much to be welcomed. So too is its willingness to invest substantial sums of money in order to research what kinds of early interventions and health-led parenting support strategies are demonstrably successful in the UK context. This emphasis on the role of health visitors and midwives during pregnancy and up to age 2, together with the Government's announcement in December 2006 that child benefit will be paid to pregnant women from their 29th week of pregnancy, from 2009, show that the Government has accepted the case for beginning interventions even earlier than the 'early years', in the period before birth.

In developing its plans for 'early intervention', the Government has drawn extensively on international evidence showing the value and effectiveness of 'pre-birth' interventions. As summarised in Box 3, the Nurse Family Partnership programme in the US has built up a strong and reliable body of evidence demonstrating the efficacy of structured programmes of home visits by specially trained nurses to disadvantaged pregnant women and new mothers.[12] Not only has the programme amassed evidence of the efficacy of structured home-visits through its randomised control trials, it has also collected data which demonstrates the value of visits by registered nurses as compared to 'paraprofessional' care-givers, who lack the same level of training and expertise.

Box 3: Research evidence from the Nurse Family Partnership Programme [13]

The Nurse-Family Partnership programme developed by David Olds began working with first-time, low-income pregnant women and new mothers in Elmira, New York three decades ago. The original study has since been replicated in geographically and ethnically diverse settings, with subsequent trials beginning in Memphis, Tennessee in 1987 and Denver, Colorado in 1994.

The evaluation studies have continued over time, charting the long-term outcomes for mothers and children involved in each of the three trials. Consistent positive effects include: improved prenatal health; fewer childhood injuries; fewer subsequent pregnancies; increased intervals between births; increased maternal employment; and improved school readiness.

Furthermore, by undertaking randomised control trials, the research team have not only been able to compare and contrast the outcomes of home-visited mothers and children with those of the control group, they have also been able to investigate whether there are differences in outcomes for participants visited by paraprofessionals as compared to trained nurses. In the Denver study, 735 first-time mothers were randomly assigned into three roughly-equal groups: a control group, a group visited by registered nurses, and a group visited by paraprofessionals – caregivers educated to high school rather than degree level. The results of the Denver study showed that while the nurse-visited mothers and children experienced important differences in outcomes, as compared to the control group, the paraprofessional-visited group displayed no such improvements. With a couple of exceptions (better child interaction and some reported reduction in psychological distress), the outcomes of those visited by paraprofessionals showed virtually no differences from the control group, who received no home visits at all.

Perhaps the most important lesson to be learned from the Nurse Family Partnership programme relates to the decision by the programme's founder, David Olds, to protect the integrity of the model, by refusing to 'roll out' the model on a limited budget, which would have required cost-cutting changes to the original version, such as using caregivers who lacked the same specialist knowledge and training as nurses.[14]

The key lesson for the implementation of the *Action Plan* in the UK, then, is that effective early years interventions come at a price. Above all, the Government should avoid the temptation of trying to emulate the success of resource-intensive programmes (such as the Nurse Family Partnership programmes) on an inadequate budget. This would also risk losing those very successes that made the original programme cost-effective in the first place. Adequate investment is not only a necessary condition of success, it is also the only guarantee that money invested will actually be returned. It may well be that the kinds of "trailblazing practical approaches" the Government envisages here will come at a higher cost than the £7 million that has been allocated to fund 10 health-led parenting support intervention projects from pre-birth to age 2.[15]

While the Government is committed to promoting "the upskilling of midwives, health visitors and commissioners to support early years interventions" and to developing "commissioning guidance to encourage the spread of best practice nationally", [16] it needs to do more to meet the shortage in specially trained health visitors and midwives, and to reverse recent cuts in Sure Start facilities and services.

As stated above, the goal should be to rebalance maternal care services, to reduce the average number of antenatal visits during pregnancy, and to release resources for investment in specialist training for staff who work with the most disadvantaged groups of women. More focused early support, as provided through Sure Start projects and centres, has the added advantaged of helping to increase the take up of high quality childcare at the next stage of the life course, but it needs to be extended to those low income and disadvantaged women and families living outside areas of deprivation, who may not qualify for this type of support.

6 | Socio-economic causes of ill-health: narrowing the gap in income, status and wealth

To be effective in promoting maternal and infant health, we need to understand and treat not just the direct causes of ill health (notably smoking and poor diet), but also the *causes* of the causes. As Richard Wilkinson and Michael Marmot have argued, we need to attend to the social determinants of health – that is, to socio-economic factors such as inequalities in income, wealth and social status, which lie at the heart of long-standing social inequalities in health outcomes and health behaviour.[1]

Understanding the socio-economic causes of maternal ill-health, and poor foetal development, is particularly important, because it reminds us of the wider set of factors which affect health outcomes, and so helps us move away from a characterisation of the 'problem' as a purely personal or behavioural phenomenon. Rather than assuming that pregnant women bear sole responsibility for the health of the baby before birth, as policy makers and commentators are wont to do, we need to understand the wider set of factors which constrain and impact on women's health behaviour.

We argue that given the very clear evidence linking poor nutrition to lack of income and deprivation, a very strong case can be made for additional financial support during pregnancy, not only to help pregnant women to afford the kind of healthy and balanced diet that is so important both to maternal health and well-being and to the healthy growth and development of the baby *in utero*, but also to help alleviate the many problems associated with stress caused by financial worries and insecurity

Crucially, addressing the social causes of ill-health is not a matter just of targeting additional resources at low-income or low-status groups, important though this is: the Government ultimately needs to consider a more far-reaching set of measures. These include policies to redress low wages, poor housing, social deprivation, lack of social contact or social networks and poor job opportunities – all of which threaten maternal health – along with action to reduce inequalities in the overall distribution of income, wealth and social status which are at the root of persistent, life-time, health inequalities.

6.1 The importance of maternal health prior to conception

Anti-poverty campaigners in the UK have expressed particular anxiety in recent years about the paucity of adult benefit rates, and of the inadequacy of financial provision for women who become pregnant for the first time whilst on income support.[2] As well as falling below the poverty line, the level of adult benefit for people without work falls well below the level calculated for minimal living standards. This is deeply worrying, since the health of women prior to conception is ultimately just as important to healthy foetal development as maternal health during pregnancy. Low income impacts on maternal and infant health not only because affordability is a key barrier to a healthy diet, but also because of the toll taken on women's health and well-being, creating levels of stress which then have further repercussions for the healthy development of the baby during pregnancy. It follows that there is an urgent need to increase financial support during the early stages of pregnancy and also prior to conception, especially for women on the lowest incomes, and to address the anomaly of varying benefit levels for mothers of different ages.

These concerns are multiplied in the case of women receiving income support who become pregnant in their teens and early twenties, because benefit levels are lower for younger women. While a lone woman aged 25 and over receives £57.45 a week, young women aged 18 to 24 who becomes pregnant with their first baby will have been living on £45.50 a week.[3] Very young women are at even greater risk of poor nutritional status, according to research which shows that the diets of teenagers are poorer nutritionally.[4] This situation is not helped by the very low benefit levels for 16 and 17 year olds on income support, of only £34.60 a week, while those under the age of 16 who are living with their parents will have to rely on what their parents can afford to give them, or what they can earn for themselves outside of school hours.[5]

The low levels of income support for single adults, young people in particular, is especially worrying, as recent analysis of the Millennium Cohort Study reveals that 74 per cent of lone mothers, 69 per cent of lone mothers having their first baby and 80 per cent of lone mothers under 18 were on income support (at nine months after birth, which was the time at which the interview took place).[6]

6.2 Proposals for increasing financial support prior to birth

In this context, the recent announcement of changes to the system of financial support for pregnant women, which for the first time will see child benefit paid from the 29th week of pregnancy, is particularly welcome. The proposal, which will take effect from April 2009, is a development of Labour's 'Early Years' strategy, which signals the Government's broad acceptance of the case for increased support in the crucial 'pre-birth' period.

By choosing to extend the payment of a universal benefit such as Child Benefit, rather than through one of the other options for increasing financial support during pregnancy (e.g. through means-tested benefits such as income support or tax credits), the

Government sensibly opted for a proposal with high political and public acceptability, which avoids the problems of social stigma and low take-up associated with means-tested benefits. As with child benefit in its current form, which achieves near-universal take-up rates (97 per cent), take-up of child benefit during pregnancy is likely to be very high.

And yet, while the broad appeal of increasing a universal benefit such as Child Benefit will help build public support for this kind of 'pre-birth' intervention, additional resources will arguably still be needed to assist the most disadvantaged groups, especially earlier in pregnancy and even prior to conception.

Timing of financial support

The decision to extend Child Benefit to the 29th week of pregnancy makes sense on practical and administrative grounds. Conveniently, the timing of the increase overlaps with the start of Maternity Leave, thereby simplifying the process of administration as it will be possible to use the same form to provide proof of pregnancy for both Maternity Leave and Child Benefit.

Helping pregnant women to access a nutritionally adequate diet during the last trimester is essential for the physical growth of the baby, as this is the time at which the foetus grows faster than any other. Although the needs of individual women will vary depending on how active they are, extra energy is required at this stage, with a recommended increase of 200 kcals a day in the last three months of pregnancy. The extension of Child Benefit to the latter stages of pregnancy will therefore provide a useful additional source of income to help meet the costs of extra food at this stage of foetal development.

But the importance of an adequate diet and nutrition is by no means confined to the latter stages of pregnancy: maternal health and nutrition in the early stages of pregnancy and also prior to conception is critical for the healthy development of the embryo. To provide the full range of nutrients for herself and her growing baby, pregnant women need to have access to a healthy and varied diet throughout their pregnancies, and particularly in the first trimester, when the embyo is formed through the multiplication and differentiation of body cells into various organ systems.[7]

Adequate resources are needed, then, not just to meet the costs of any additional food that pregnant women will consume in the later stages of pregnancy, but to help pregnant women and future mothers to access the kind of healthy and varied diet that is needed to provide her and her developing baby with the full range of nutrients for foetal growth. As affordability is the key (though by no means the only) barrier to a healthy diet for people on low income, there remains an urgent need to provide additional financial support for low-income women throughout pregnancy, particularly in the early stages and also prior to conception. Thus, while we welcome the announcement of an increase in universal Child Benefit from the 29th week of pregnancy, beginning in 2009, we argue that this proposal needs to be supplemented with additional support targeted at those in greatest financial need, who have the greatest risk of experiencing poor pregnancy outcomes.

Policy options for increasing financial support

What, then, is the appropriate policy response to the problem of poor maternal health and poor nutritional status, especially amongst pregnant women and future mothers on low incomes?

One possible option would be to extend Child Benefit even earlier into pregnancy. However, not only would this be more complex to administer than the current proposal, it also raises difficult ethical questions regarding the status of the foetus prior to 24 weeks (the legal abortion limit).[8] Arguably, the priority is to target any additional public resources on the lowest income groups, to help meet the costs of an adequate (though modest) diet during pregnancy, which the Food Commission estimates as £20 per week.[9] Given the strong connections between poor diet and lack of income, it is important to target any additional spending most directly on those in greatest need, and also to provide extra financial resources earlier in pregnancy. This could be done in a number of ways, for example by extending child tax credit eligibility to pregnancy, as proposed by Maternity Alliance, or by introducing a 'pregnancy premium' to increase the amount of benefit received by pregnant women on income support, as recommended by the Fabian Commission on Life Chances and Child Poverty.[10]

Nevertheless, there are drawbacks with any such proposal. The challenge is to ensure that any additional financial support is taken up by all those entitled to receive it, and that it is received early enough to make a difference in the critical first weeks after conception – the difficulty being that any financial support for pregnant women will encounter a delay whilst pregnancy is confirmed. Moreover, given the importance of women's health and nutrition prior to conception as well as during pregnancy, the lowest-income groups would benefit from additional financial support before as well as during pregnancy. Offering financial support to women who are trying for a baby would obviously be extremely difficult to regulate and liable to fraudulent claims. In addition, this kind of support would not benefit those women whose pregnancies are unplanned, who are more likely to come from low-income, nutritionally vulnerable groups.

While the Labour Government has prioritised increases in benefits for children and families since 1997, benefit rates for adults not in paid work have been allowed to fall further behind average earnings.[11] Adult benefit rates are now far below the Government's own poverty line (60 per cent of contemporary median income), as well as falling below a level adequate to maintain minimum standards of living, as calculated by the Centre for Research in Social Policy and the Family Budget Unit.[12] It follows that there is an urgent need for the Government to increase adult benefit rates to adequacy levels, as well as needing to review its benefit uprating policy to ensure that financial support holds its value, relative to societal living standards, as recommended by Lisa Harker in her recent report for the Department of Work and Pensions.[13] Ensuring adequate levels of financial support for those on benefits would not only recognise the needs of the adults themselves, but would also help protect children yet to be born from the effects of poverty.

Perhaps the most urgent priority, however, is to increase support for young prospective mothers who are so vulnerable to income poverty, particularly those under the age of 25 who receive lower benefit levels. As teenagers have the highest risk of all age groups of having an underweight baby, more needs to be done to ensure that young prospective parents have sufficient income to achieve a nutritionally balanced diet and to alleviate the negative effects of stress associated with very low income. The lower benefit levels currently received by young people under the age of 25 is an anomaly that urgently needs to be addressed. Raising income support levels for young people would help to promote the health of prospective parents, as well as being a relatively efficient way of targeting young lone mothers, as 60 per cent of 18-24 year old income support claimants are lone parents, and 74 per cent of 18-24 year old lone parents are claiming income support.[14]

Recommendation 4: Increase financial support before and during pregnancy

Adequate financial support is needed before and during pregnancy to promote the health of pregnant women and prospective parents, particularly young pregnant women and parents-to-be, who currently receive lower levels of income support than those aged 25 and above. The first priority for Government is therefore to end the current disparity in benefit rates between people of different ages, so that all 18 to 24 year olds are entitled to receive the full adult rate. Over the medium term, the Government must commit to increase the rate of adult benefit, to bring it into line with the minimum income required to meet basic needs, and to ensure that benefit levels are uprated in line with general living standards. This would not only recognise the needs of the adults themselves, but would also help protect children yet to be born from the effects of poverty.

"

7 | Strategies to reduce low birth weight: younger and older mothers

7.1 Strategies to reduce the incidence of low birth weight amongst teenage parents

Teenage parents have the highest risk of all parents of having a low birth weight baby, while the teenage pregnancy rate in Britain is the highest in Europe – a trend that the Government is anxious to reverse. In fact, in the 1970s, the UK had similar teenage birth rates to other European countries, but while rates elsewhere declined over time, figures for the UK barely moved. Since 1997 the Labour Government has committed itself to addressing the problem, setting out plans for a preventative overall health strategy,[1] alongside measures to target potential teenage mothers from at-risk groups before they become pregnant.[2] A key part of the Teenage Pregnancy Strategy (TPS), launched in 1999, is to improve information and advice on sexual health and access to contraception: the ten year programme includes provision to offer new training on sex education for teachers and schools' inspection on the subject as well as guidance for health professionals on offering advice and contraception.

More recently, the TPS has been updated to focus more directly on 21 local authority "hotspots" with the highest levels of teenage pregnancy, rather than on a nationwide programme, and to acknowledge the importance of a wider approach to consider underlying causes including poverty, exclusion and poor education. [3] A key component of this strategy is not only to target areas where teenagers are most at risk of becoming pregnant, but also to target teenagers in those areas who are most at risk. New emphasis has been given to offering advice to young men about the consequences of sex as well as a plan to give sex and relationship advice to teenagers excluded from school. The Government has also signalled that it will set out new measures in a future document to improve educational attainment, attendance at school and post-16 participation.

The broadening of the Government's approach, to consider the underlying causes of early parenthood, including poverty, social exclusion and poor education, is an important step, because educational outcomes which are strongly associated with material deprivation, such as low educational attainment, or disengagement from the school system, are also likely to be important mechanisms through which teenage motherhood confers later life disadvantage.[4] The shift is also in line with more recent research which suggests that the negative effects associated with teenage parenting may not be due to early motherhood itself, but rather reflect the pre-existing disadvantage of those young people who typically become pregnant as teenagers. In policy terms, this means that policies focused primarily on reducing teenage conception rates may not be as effective in improving young people's life chances as longer-term strategies to address the underlying socio-economic disadvantage which blights their lives.

Efforts to engage and improve the attainment of young people 'at risk' of early pregnancy will need to begin early, as many of those who are at highest risk of becoming teenage mothers begin missing school long before they become pregnant. Research has shown that less than half of teenage mothers were good attendees at school before conception.[5] For many young mothers disengagement from education came well before the pregnancy. Hence, "the decision to become a young mother may in part be a direct result of leaving school young, and not the other way round".[6]

A number of indicators for girls at 10 years old strongly predict the likelihood of becoming a teenage mother.[7] These include having a conduct disorder, having poor reading ability, being in a family in receipt of benefits, being in social housing and having parents who had low aspirations.

The same study finds that the odds are higher for those young women whose own parents left school at 16, who lived in a lone parent family, whose father was in social classes IV and V, and whose own mother was a teenage mother. The highest five of these factors combined increased the odds of becoming a teenage mother by 31 per cent. In theory, these indicators could be used to identify girls age 10 at greatest risk of having an early pregnancy, who could then be offered extra forms of support, including learning, emotional and social support, for example through peer support, a learning mentor, or other members of the non-teaching staff. The challenge in practice for this kind of targeted support, however, would be how to identify and support 'at risk' individuals without labelling or stigmatising those young people. (Clearly, it would hardly help encourage participation in such schemes if they were publicly labelled as aimed at preventing teenage pregnancy). Much depends, then, on the professionalism and sensitivity of the support worker, who would need specialist training and experience in building up positive relationships with young people.

Improving sex, relationship and health education in schools: the role of school nurses

Although the provision of information and advice on contraception and sexual health has been a core part of the TPS since its inception, the generally slow rates of progress on reducing the teenage conception rate indicates that further steps need to be taken to improve the teaching of sex and relationship education (SRE) in schools.

Inevitably, perhaps, schools have been expected to address an ever-widening list of social and personal issues over the last thirty years or so, in response to growing societal concerns about health and behavioural problems amongst young people, such as drug and alcohol use, crime and sexual behaviour.[8] The impulse to charge schools with responsibility for addressing such problems is hardly surprising, given the captive audience within the classroom. But there are concerns about the capacity of schools – and teacher trainers – to cover the array of topics that fall within the domain of personal, social and health education (PSHE) or 'preparation for adult life', due to a lack of specialist teachers, and because the subject is not compulsory and not assessed, so is less likely to be taken seriously either by staff or pupils. As one lecturer in education remarked, "There is rarely room in these extremely crowded PGCE programmes for more than one session (and sometimes not even that) on any one of the multiplying and ever-changing 'priorities' that government agencies and an array of pressure groups want such courses to address – usually 'urgently'".[9]

One way to improve sex and relationship education (SRE) and health education in schools would be to prioritise training and resources to provide a medically trained individual, such as a school nurse, on site as part of the school team (see case study).

Box 4: Case Study: Bracknell Forest

Teenage pregnancy rates in Bracknell Forest area have fallen significantly since the Teenage Pregnancy Strategy was set up in 1999.[10] Every secondary school in the area now has a drop-in centre where young people can go for advice in a neutral environment, while the Teenage Pregnancy team also run training on sexual education for teachers to help them feel more confident with the subject.

Two schools have a weekly sexual health clinic on site during term time, where a doctor, youth worker and school nurse are all on hand to offer different types of advice about everything from sexual health, sexually transmitted infections and relationships with their parents to relationships with their boyfriend or girlfriend. The service is only available to students in year 10 and 11, but it is considered to be successfully striking a balance between offering help in an educational environment and having experts on hand. "Young people will talk about all sorts of things to us. They come and it's confidential. Confidentiality is huge," said Teenage Pregnancy Strategy leader Lorraine Parker. Noting the gap between teenagers and their parents when it comes to talking about sex, Parker is keen to look at peer education as a possible further avenue to improve the service: "Young people listen to young people," she says.

In focus group discussions conducted for this project with teenage mothers, there was general agreement that it would be better for sex education to be taught by someone with a medical background, "who is not a teacher", who would be "less easy to embarrass" and who students "might take a bit more seriously".

As MP and GP Howard Stoate says, the school nurse would be the "ideal health champion in schools".[11] Stoate advocates giving school nurses a key role in assessing the health needs of pupils and putting together moves to improve their general health. There are lessons to be learned here from Finland, where school nurses specially trained to work with young people are the first port of call on most health issues.[12] In a study comparing sexual health policies in Finland and Scotland, Alison Hosie concludes that school nurses have a significant role in Finland's sexual education strategy, and its relatively low rates of teenage pregnancy,[13] as school nurses create a separate communication link with students, independent of teachers and parents, and are often seen as more approachable. Finally, in Finnish schools, pupils are encouraged to take responsibility for their own health, by organising appointments with the school nurse themselves, rather than only attending the doctor with their parents, as often occurs in England and Scotland.

More can be done, therefore, to integrate the pre-birth agenda into the programme of health education in schools, by increasing the number of school nurses and giving them an enhanced role. At present there is currently about one nurse to every ten schools in England.[14] Over time, the number of school nurses should be increased to allow a school nurse on site in every primary and secondary school at least once a week, with a medium- to long-term goal of providing a school nurse for every school. The introduction of more school nurses into UK schools could help improve the health education of all pupils, and, with additional training, help to identify potential at-risk teenage parents. By working with 'at risk' girls, school nurses could also help them to improve their own health and nutrition, and so improve the chances of their having a normal weight baby, in the event of their becoming pregnant.

Thus, instead of calling for an additional range of responsibilities to be added to the workload of teachers, we argue that some of those responsibilities could be relieved through an extension in the number of school nurses. Working alongside other non-teaching staff (such as learning mentors), school nurses can provide additional sources of contact and support within the school setting, but distinct from the teaching staff.

Recommendation 5: A school nurse for every school

The number of school nurses needs to be increased, with the ultimate aim of providing one nurse for every school, to improve general health outcomes as well as to promote pupils' sex and relationship education as appropriate at a younger age. School nurses would be the first port of call for young people on many health issues, providing additional sources of contact and support within the school setting, but distinct from teaching staff. For the most vulnerable young women, school nurses should work alongside other non-teaching staff, such as learning mentors, to provide more intensive forms of emotional and relationship support, as well as helping young people improve their health outcomes.

Adequacy of support services for younger parents and those at risk of early pregnancy

There is also an urgent need to look at the quality of support services available for young fathers and mothers and for young people at risk of early parenthood.[15]

The Department for Education and Skills reports greatest success in reversing teenage pregnancy trends where senior local figures have been committed to the Teenage Pregnancy programme. It has identified the need for dedicated advisors for teenage parents, the provision of Sure Start Plus and Childrens' Centres in all areas and dedicated housing for all teenage parents under 18 who cannot live at home. However, while the need for specialist provision for teenage parents and continuity of care is now widely recognised in principle, there is evidence that the same high standards are not always being achieved in practice.

Specialist training for health professionals working with young parents is crucial, as teenage parents have particular needs in terms of family support services: for example, research shows that they are the group most likely "to find it difficult to establish a good relationship with a health visitor and are more likely to use friends and family as a source of information and advice," whilst also being particularly concerned about finances and childcare.[16]

The manner in which pregnant women and their partners are treated by health and medical staff is clearly important, whatever their age. Of the young mothers interviewed for this project, those who had experience of a specially trained 'teen pregnancy' midwife were enthusiastic in their praise: "She was less judgemental. You knew she was for people in your situation. She was really, really nice."

There is also an urgent need to secure funding for antenatal and post-natal classes specifically for young parents. In one residential centre for young mothers that we visited, none of the three teenage mothers interviewed had attended ante-natal classes more than once. It was common for younger mothers to report feeling out of place in their antenatal class, because it was composed mainly of older women: as one teenager remarked, "I felt uncomfortable as there were so many older women there."

In addition, research suggests that teenage fathers are less likely to attend antenatal classes than older fathers because of a fear of feeling embarrassed, not feeling comfortable in groups or believing that they would not fit in with the other people who attended.[17]"In general there are few support networks for new fathers and this is exacerbated by the fact that often fathers' primary role is seen to be to support of the mother of the baby".[18] It is therefore important to stress the importance of ante-natal and post-natal support groups targeted specifically at young fathers.

While good progress has been made on integrating maternity care with early years services through Children's Centres and Sure Start Plus, problems of 'short-termism' remain. In particular, there are problems arising from the short term nature of many sources of funding for posts such as specially trained 'teenage pregnancy' midwives, nursery nurses and family support workers. Staff in one Children's Centre that we visited, for example, reported that pressure on resources had led to a number of family support workers being cut over the last twelve months, putting at threat the future of well-established support services, such as ante-natal and post-natal groups for young mothers and fathers. Clearly there are still flaws in the current system when projects with a proven track record are threatened with closure due to insecure funding. The challenge in such cases is not that of identifying what works, but protecting the funding for specific projects, to ensure that the specialist support services targeted at young men and women can be continued.

7.2 Reducing low birth weight amongst older parents

Older women (aged 40+) also face an enhanced risk having a baby with a low birth weight, and yet the average age at which women give birth to their first child has been rising over time. A number of factors appear to responsible for this trend, including the "rising age at completing full-time education; changes in relationship patterns; later age at initiation of co-residential unions; women's greater propensity to have employment careers; and a general increase in lifestyle and standard of living aspirations".[19] If these factors are contributing to women's decisions to delay parenthood, should policy makers consider measures to enable women and their partners to exercise greater choice over when to start a family?

The decision of when to have a family is of course a private one, in which, it might be argued, Government should not interfere (beyond perhaps ensuring that adequate information and advice is available to those considering starting a family, whatever their age). However, the Government may well have a role in ameliorating those factors that can prevent women from starting their families earlier in their lives. This, in turn, may decrease the number of babies born to older mothers, at risk of a lower birth weight.

Critics might say that there are no grounds for intervention here, as prospective parents need to weigh up the health risks for themselves, depending on their own circumstances. However, the Teenage Pregnancy Strategy shows that there is a precedent for Government action to discourage pregnancy at less 'optimum' times in life. Just as government action to encourage very young women to delay having children until they are older is combined with policies to support those young people who do become pregnant in their teens, government action to remove obstacles to women and couples starting a family in their twenties and early thirties could be taken alongside measures to ensure proper support and health advice to anyone wanting to start a family later in life.

While the starting point must be to respect women's and couples' right to decide the best arrangement for themselves – whether staying at home or returning to work, the question is whether we as a society can do more to assist family life and to ease the pressure on women and their partners. With a range of economic and social factors pushing people to start families later, should employers, public service providers, higher education institutions, and so on, be taking measures to facilitate earlier parenting and to help avoid some of the health risks associated with having a baby later in life? If so, what type of measures might be appropriate?

* * *

Action to tackle the barriers that prevent women from starting families earlier in their lives is often inhibited by the unfair and unhelpful perception that women are trying to "have it all" by combining a career and a family.[20] This view betrays an assumption that it is natural for men to work and be a parent, but that women are somehow jeopardising family life, and the welfare of their children, by attempting to do the same. This type of view also tends to present the decision of when to have children as an individual choice, made by women, without considering that men are playing a part in those decisions too, and without regard to the wider set of constraints and factors which shape and limit people's choices.

In focus group interviews conducted for this project, we asked some (relatively) 'older' mothers, who had had their first child in their late thirties or forties, for their reaction to the charge that women today want to 'have it all'. A common reaction was to reject the idea of a 'one-size-fits-all' model and to assert that different parenting or working decisions will make sense to different women:

> How does one define having it all? A stay-at-home mother may very well be happy and think herself having it all so may a career woman who sends her child to childcare. (47 year old woman who had her first child age 41)

Many of our focus group participants, both the 'younger' mothers and the 'older' mothers, also rejected the idea that there was a 'perfect age' at which to have children. As one older mother observed:

> It is so dependent on the individual's health and other circumstances: economically, emotionally, it is better to have a child when you're older, because you are more stable financially and more ready to settle down. But you'd be less likely then to know your grandchildren".(41 year old mother who had her first child age 40)

None of the participants (who with one exception were university graduates) had considered starting a family whilst still in full-time education. Indeed, two women revealed that they had become pregnant whilst at university, but had chosen to have an abortion rather than continue the pregnancy. One 'older' mother, who works in a professional occupation, described how the pressure to complete her studies has influenced her attitude towards having children:

I was a student for most of my twenties, so it wasn't an option then. I know people who had babies when they were students, but they found it too difficult so had to drop out. I knew I couldn't start a family until I'd finished my studies, because if I'd had a baby I might have had to drop out too. (37 year woman who had her first child aged 35)

Although the responses were not characterised by any single pattern or circumstance, the most frequently given reason for not having a baby earlier was that "I hadn't found the right partner". A number of interviewees said they might have started a family earlier if they had met the right person before, while several had been married in their twenties, but it had not worked out, so they had waited to start a family until later in their thirties, when they had remarried. As these 'older' mothers remarked: "It was important to be in a relationship. It was really that I didn't meet the right person earlier"; "Basically, I was waiting until I was sure it was the right man to start a family with"; "It was quite straightforward for me: I wanted to have a child in a loving relationship."

The importance of meeting the right person is supported by evidence from an on-line survey of 327 'older' mothers, which found that the most popular reason for "leaving it until later in life to start a family" was the lack of a suitable partner earlier on.[21]

Figure 7: Online survey

Why did you leave it until later in life to start trying for a baby?

Lack of suitable partner earlier on	41.3 %
Didn't, but wanted baby with new partner	11.6 %
Partner not ready	3.7 %
I wasn't ready	9.8 %
Infertility	7.0 %
Career concerns	3.1 %
Financial reasons	3.9%
Never thought I'd want a baby!	4.7 %
Other	4.9 %

Source: webpollcentral.com

Thus, rather than trying to 'have it all', many women simply want to establish a stable family unit and a secure financial and employment base before trying to start a family. A 'blame culture' in the media is therefore particularly unfair, as well as being unhelpful, as it reduces a complex set of circumstances, and of economic and social pressures, to an individual decision.

While policy and media discussions need to stop presenting decisions or 'choices' about when to start a family as a purely individual matter, can we collectively do anything to facilitate earlier parenting? What kinds of measures might be taken to increase the options available to women and couples?

First of all, it is worth stressing that any such action must start from the position of respecting the right of women and couples to make their own decisions about when to start a family. The Government's approach must be to enable men and women to exercise greater choice over when to start a family.

At the very least, Government has a responsibility to ensure that women and men of child-bearing age have an adequate understanding of the health and fertility risks associated with conception over the age of 40. Although we cannot generalise from our focus groups, the 'older' mothers we spoke to were certainly very familiar with the general health problems and fertility risks associated with age. There was much less awareness, however, of the enhanced risk of having a low birth weight baby for women in their forties, and of the health risks faced by underweight babies. For example, one mother, aged 47, who had her first child at 41, said that because she was an older mother, she sought out health information about risks and was particularly aware that Down's Syndrome problems could occur. But while she knew it was important that the mother be in good health, she said she "wasn't particularly aware of low birth weight being a factor". These responses indicate that Government agencies could possibly do more to promote awareness of the increased risk of having a low birth weight baby for older women.

Beyond increasing the amount of information available to men and women, more, arguably, needs to be done to remove disincentives to parenting, such as the loss of earnings associated with childbirth. The challenge for policy makers is to reduce the 'fertility penalty' to women's lifetime earnings associated with childbirth, which occurs because women often return to work at lower pay levels, while some parents, mostly women, drop out of the labour market entirely. This fertility penalty was reported in our focus group interviews: as expressed by one 'older' mother: "I want to go back to work, but all the flexible jobs are badly paid and at a much lower level than the one I was working at before. It would be difficult to make it financially worthwhile." As Dixon and Margo (2006) observe, the most cost effective way to reduce the 'fertility penalty' would be to focus on improving childcare provision and parental leave.[22]

The Labour Government has already taken significant steps to assist working families, through investment in childcare and the 'early years' and by making changes to parental leave arrangements and entitlements, with extensions to paid maternity leave and the introduction of paid paternity leave for the first time.[23]

Interestingly, the introduction of these family-friendly measures has been linked to the recent upturn in fertility rates: after reaching an all-time low of 1.63 in 2001, the total fertility rate in the UK (calculated by measuring the number of births in a year relative to the number of women of childbearing age) rose in 2002, 2003 and 2004.[24]

But more can still be done to relieve the pressures on working parents to balance work and family life, which remain considerable. Amongst our focus group participants, there was a strong sense that there is still a long way to go to change working practices and workplace culture, with a common view that employers are not flexible and open to part-time working.

Greater investment and commitment to family-friendly working practices is needed from employers as well as well as Government, in order to extend opportunities for flexible working and to provide more accessible, affordable and flexible childcare. Proposals for more flexible working arrangements for new parents could include a right to flexible working for parents of children under 2 (as opposed to the current right to request flexible working). This suggestion received strong support from the older mothers in our focus groups, many of whom expressed huge frustrations with their experience of trying to balance family and working life. More affordable and flexible childcare was another priority for many of the mothers we interviewed.

The case for further government action in this area is supported by international data, which reveals broad differences in fertility rates in countries with different patterns of employment and childcare provision. The highest rates of fertility are found in the 'Nordic' countries of Sweden, Denmark and Norway which have gone furthest in promoting gender equality in the work place, with more 'family-friendly' working practices such as flexible working, and more accessible and affordable childcare.[25] By contrast, lower fertility rates are found in Mediterranean countries such as Spain and Portugal which are characterised by a longer transition to adulthood and financial independence, including more time spent living in the family home. In addition, a shortage of part-time jobs in Spain means that it is more difficult for mothers to combine paid employment with caring for children.[26] Moreover, international studies provide evidence that 'family friendly' policies can have an impact on the age at which mothers have their first baby, with the introduction of more flexible working conditions associated with a shift towards earlier childbearing.[27]

And yet, other policies intended to influence the pattern of parenting, such as financial support for parents who stay at home could have knock-on effects, which would create tension with competing policy objectives. For example, the introduction in France in 1994 of a financial incentive for one parent (in practice, almost exclusively women) to stay at home in the first three years after birth had ramifications for gender equality, as it reinforced a traditional gender division of labour, leading to a significant decrease in the proportion of women aged 20 to 40 with two children in paid work (falling from 66 per cent in 1990 to 47 per cent in 1999).[28] Any attempt to facilitate earlier parenting would need to be evaluated, therefore, against other policy priorities, such as efforts to promote gender equality at home and in the workplace, to promote women's entry or return to work in areas of high occupational segregation and to break down gender inequalities in the sharing of domestic responsibilities.

Finally, it is worth emphasising the need to address the gender imbalance in the distribution of family, domestic and caring responsibilities.[29] Far from 'having it all', until greater progress is made towards a more genuinely even share of caring responsibilities, women will continue to struggle to reconcile their desire to start a family with their right to pursue a financially and personally rewarding career.

Our focus on life chances therefore provides an important set of reasons for building on the Government's 'early years' agenda. But we also need to go further: given the preponderance of later parenthood amongst women in professional and managerial occupations, we need to look at features of these professional career structures which create pressure towards later parenting. For example, we might consider the implications of a 'pre-birth' strategy for higher education policy, as well as the role of employers and professional organisations in sectors such as law, medicine, finance, banking, and accountancy in helping rethink the career structures of professional occupations. In higher education, while the Government is investing more than ever before on additional support for mature students with children, and on fee waivers and loans for those studying part-time, the Department for Education and Skills admits that "the system (of funding and additional support) has become over-complex and difficult for students to understand and access, and an administrative burden for some institutions".[30] Two priorities for higher education policy in the short to medium term, therefore, might be to increase the number of statutory grants available for mature students with children, whilst reducing complexities in the system of application, funding and financial support.

Over the longer term, the goal might be to change the pattern of studying and training over the life course, so that there would be less onus on completing academic study and professional training before starting a family.[31] It is possible to envisage changes to the present system of medical training, for example, which puts so much pressure on female medical students to complete their years of extended academic study and clinical training before starting a family, to move towards a system where it would be easier for medical students to take a break to start a family (for example, in their mid-twenties) then return to professional training at a later stage (e.g. in their early thirties). Any such shift in training and working patterns over the life course would need to be supported by the relevant professional associations and trade unions, though government agencies and the public sector could continue to take a lead in promoting more flexible approaches to working and family life.

8 | Where do we go from here?

A vision of a better society

Being born at a low birth weight casts a long shadow over children's prospects of flourishing for the rest of their lives. So it is an obvious cause for concern that babies born to families on low incomes are significantly more likely to be born underweight than the population as a whole. Tackling this inequality – and aiming to give every child the best start in life – should be a key priority for any social justice agenda.

This pamphlet has considered some of the next steps in this emerging agenda. The policy priorities we have identified would do much to improve birth outcomes and narrow the gap in inequalities at birth. And yet, to close the social class gap in birth outcomes, it is also apparent that we need to do more than identify the next steps; we must keep in mind a broader vision of the kind of society we are trying to move towards: a society where there is adequate support for women during pregnancy; a society which is structured in a way that increases the options available to women and men to make optimal choices in family planning; and a society in which everyone – from the pregnant woman, her partner, her family and friends, her employer and society as a whole – is aware of the contribution they can make to healthy foetal development.

Beyond the specific recommendations of this report, this agenda will require further progress in a range of policy areas. We should aspire to a society in which every person who needs it is entitled to decent quality social housing and a level of financial support sufficient to achieve basic living standards; in which high quality health services, in a range of community and hospital-based settings, and integrated with forms of social support, are widely and readily available to all; and in which individuals, couples and families are able to achieve a proper balance between their working and personal lives – including through better and more affordable childcare provision, appropriate rights at work, and a more family-friendly employment culture. As well as providing adequate support for parents in the stressful and demanding time after the birth of a child and the first years of life, we also need to relieve pressures on parents-to-be, by introducing greater flexibility over the life course in patterns of study, training and employment. Finally, closing the gap in birth outcomes ultimately depends on how far we can narrow inequalities in income, wealth and social status, which lie at the heart of long-standing inequalities in people's health.

Ultimately, our vision is of a society where the circumstances of our birth, and the advantages and disadvantages which we inherit, matter much less than they do today. While we cannot imagine that the gap in people's life chances will ever vanish entirely, we need to draw confidence from what international evidence tells us about the power of progressive governments and societies to bring about change. Inequality is not an inevitable feature of life; it is within our power to ensure that children from every social background have more equal life chances, beginning from birth.

Where do we go from here?

Recommendation 1: Reduce social inequalities in access to maternity care

More needs to be done to reduce social inequalities in access to maternity care, especially through investing in specially trained nursing staff and outreach workers to help meet the needs of pregnant women most at risk of having a sick, premature or underweight baby. This extra investment could be achieved either through an increase in overall funding for maternity care, or by rebalancing antenatal services: as the UK currently aims for a relatively high number of antenatal appointments for pregnant women – 13 compared to 9 in many EU countries – the standard number of antenatal visits could be reduced without negatively affecting maternal or infant health, which would then release additional resources to focus support on the most disadvantaged groups of pregnant women.

Recommendation 2: One-to-one nursing care for the most vulnerable infants

Although the most vulnerable infants – those born sick, premature and underweight – ought to be entitled to the optimum level of neonatal care, marked shortfalls remain in nursing staff levels and in the number of specially trained nurses in neonatal care units. The Department of Health has acknowledged the need for one to one nursing for babies in neonatal intensive care (as is already the norm for adult patients in intensive care). But it has yet to make this standard of care mandatory, and so must do so as an urgent priority. To promote staff recruitment and retention, neonatal units should be encouraged to adopt more flexible ways of working and incentivised to invest in training more nurses with specialist expertise.

Recommendation 3: Make reducing low birth weight a national health and social priority

The Government must signal its determination to improve birth outcomes by making a reduction in low birth weight a national health and social priority. As part of this, a greater commitment is needed at the national level to address the paucity of knowledge about what kinds of policies can be effective in promoting maternal and infant health. To build up the evidence base on effective policy interventions, Government must demonstrate this commitment by increasing investment in rigorous research studies (for example, to encourage larger sample sizes and to fund randomised control trials).

Recommendation 4: Increase financial support before and during pregnancy

Adequate financial support is needed before and during pregnancy to promote the health of pregnant women and prospective parents, particularly young pregnant women and parents-to-be, who currently receive lower levels of income support than those aged 25 and above. The first priority for Government is therefore to end the current disparity in benefit rates between people of different ages, so that all 18 to 24 year olds are entitled to receive the full adult rate. Over the medium term, the government must commit to increase the rate of adult benefit, to bring it into line with the minimum income required to meet basic needs, and to ensure that benefit levels are uprated in line with general living standards. This would not only recognise the needs of the adults themselves, but would also help protect children yet to be born from the effects of poverty.

Recommendation 5: A school nurse for every school

The number of school nurses needs to be increased, with the ultimate aim of providing one nurse for every school, to improve general health outcomes as well as to promote pupils' sex and relationship education as appropriate at a younger age. School nurses would be the first port of call for young people on many health issues, providing additional sources of contact and support within the school setting, but distinct from teaching staff. For the most vulnerable young women, school nurses should work alongside other non-teaching staff, such as learning mentors, to provide more intensive forms of emotional and relationship support, as well as helping young people improve their health outcomes.

Recommendation 6: Develop a public and political consensus to tackle the problem

We call on each of the major political parties to acknowledge the effect of inequalities at birth in shaping life chances when setting out their social justice policy agendas, to recognise explicitly the role of wider social factors in any analysis of the causes of such inequalities, and to commit themselves to action to tackle the problem, including the other recommendations contained here. A test of each party manifesto will be what policies they propose to follow over the course of the next parliament to narrow these gaps.

References

Introduction

1   *Narrowing the Gap; the Fabian Commission on Life Chances and Child Poverty,* (Fabian Society, 2006)

Chapter 1

1   Alexander, G. (2006) Prematurity at Birth: Determinants, Consequences and Geographic Variation Appendix B, *Board on Health Sciences Policy,* pp. 501.

2   Hennessey, P. (09/10/2006) *Daily Telegraph*

3   Porter, A. (01/09/2006) *The Sun*

4   Benn, T. (05/09/2009) *BBC News Online*

Chapter 2

1   North, J. (2005) *Support from the Start: Lessons from International Early Years Policy,* London: Maternity Alliance.

2   Smith, L. *et al.* (2005) *Socio-economic Inequalities in Very Pre-term Birth Rates,* Leicester: Department of Health Sciences, University of Leicester.

3   Low birth weight is defined as less than 2,500 grams (5lb 8oz). Normal birth weight is between 2,500 and 4,500 grams (5.5lbs to 9lbs 15oz).

4   Low birth weight and preterm birth may overlap (i.e. a low birth weight infant may also be preterm) but these terms are not inter-changeable, since low birth weight can occur in a full term delivery as well as an early birth.

5   Small for gestational age' (SGA) is another commonly used indicator of foetal growth restriction, and is usually defined as less than the 10th percentile of birth weight for gestational age.

6   Babies born within the normal range of weight for their age are defined as 'appropriate for gestational age'.

7   Confidential Enquiry into Maternal and Child Health (2006)
        Improving the health of mothers, babies and children, First
        Interim Report, London: CEMACH, p. 11.

8   Collingwood Bakeo, A. and Clarke, L. (2006) *Risk factors for
        low birth weight based on birth registration and census informa
        tion, England and Wales 1981-2000.*

9   For example, analysis of data for 10,845 males and females
        born during 3-9 March 1958, with information on birth weight,
        social class and cognitive tests, shows that the outcome of all
        childhood cognitive tests and educational achievements
        improved significantly with increasing birth weight. Jefferis, B.,
        Power, C. and Hertzman, C. (2002) 'Birth weight, childhood
        socio-economic environment, and cognitive development in the
        1958 British birth cohort study', *British Medical Journal*, Volume
        325, 10 August 2002.

10   Using data from the British cohort studies, Currie and Hyson
        (1999) show that low birth weight has a persistence negative
        effect on a range of longer-term outcomes, being associated
        with less completed education, lower earnings and lower prob
        abilities of employment at age 33. Similar findings have been
        found in studies in Norway, Canada and California (Black *et al.*
        2005; Oreopolous *et al.* 2006; Royer 2005, cited in Currie, J.
        and Hyson, R. (1999) 'Is the impact of health shocks cushioned
        by socio-economic status: The case of low birth weight',
        American Economic Review 92(5), pp. 1308-34.

11   Page, A. (2002) *Changing Times: Support for Parents and
        Families During Pregnancy and the First Twelve Months*,
        London: ippr.

12   Alexander, G. (2006) Prematurity at Birth: Determinants,
        Consequences and Geographic Variation Appendix B, *Board on
        Health Sciences Policy*, pp. 501 – 535.

13   Office National Statistics (1988-2006) *Social Trends*, London:
        HMSO.

14   ONS 2004.

15   Moser *et al.* (2003), p. 688, cited in Dex, S. and Joshi, H. (2005) *Children of the 21st Century: From birth to nine months*, Bristol: The Policy Press, ONS 2004.

16   Dezateux *et al.* (2005), p. 138, cited in Dex and Joshi (2005).

17   Office National Statistics (2004) *Social Trends 34,* HMSO.

18   Maher and Macfarlane 2004, cited in Jayaweera (2005), p 112

19   MacFarlane, A. and Mugford, M. (2000) *Birth Counts: statistics of Pregnancy and Childbirth*, Volume 1 London: TSO; Collingwood Bakeo and Clarke (2006), p. 15.

Chapter 3

1   Attree, P. (2005) 'Low-income mothers, nutrition and health: a systematic review of qualitative evidence', *Maternal and Child Nutrition 1 (4), 227-240.*

2   Under normal conditions, foetal growth occurs through three distinct processes at the cellular level (formation of the organ systems through cell multiplication and differentiation, cell hyperplasia and cell hypertrophy), which roughly correspond to development in the first, second and third trimester respec -tively. Foetal growth restriction (IUGR) occurs when cell hyper-plasia and hypertrophy in the second and third trimesters take place in a sub-optimal manner, resulting in deficient growth in the foetal weight, size and maturation of the foetal metabo-lism.

3   Health Development Agency (2003) *'Prevention of Low Birth Weight: Assessing the effectiveness of smoking cessation and nutritional interventions'*. Available at: http://www.hda.nhs.uk/Documents/low_birth_weight.pdf

4   Smoking during pregnancy may also increase the risk of atten-tion deficit disorder, deficits in motor skills and perception and reduced educational achievement. Rowe, R. *et al.* (2003) *Access to Care for Low Income Childbearing Women:*

Background: Inequalities in Mother and Baby Health in England, Oxford University: NPEU and Maternity Alliance.

5   Kramer 1987, cited in HDA (2003), p. 2 – conclusion of a meta-analysis of 277 English and French language studies published between 1970 and 1984

6   *Infant Feeding Survey 2000*, for Department of Health, Scottish Executive, National Assembly for Wales and Department of Health, Social Services and Public Safety in Northern Ireland.

7   Dallison J, Lobstein T. (1995) *Poor expectations. Poverty and undernourishment in pregnancy*, London: NCH Action for Children & Maternity Alliance; Wynn, S. W., Wynn, A.H.A., Doyle, W., and Crowford, M.A. (1994) 'The association of maternal social class with maternal diet and the dimensions of babies in a population of London women', *Nutrition and Health*, vol. 9, pp. 303-315..

8   Daniels, Cynthia R. (1999): 'Fathers, Mothers and Fetal Harm: Rethinking Gender Difference and Reproductive Responsibility', in *Fetal Subjects, Feminist Positions*, ed. Morgan, Lynn M. and Michaels, Meredith W., University of Pennsylvania Press: Philadelphia.

9   For a review, see Olshan, Andrew F. and Faustman, Elaine M. (1993) 'Male-Mediated Developmental Toxicity', *Reproductive Toxicology 7*, pp. 191-202.

10 Rowe, R. and Garcia, J. (2003) *Access to Care for Low Income Childbearing Women: Evidence on Access to Maternity and Infant Care in England*, Oxford University National Perinatal Epidemiology Unit (NPEU) and Maternity Alliance.

11 Rowe and Garcia (2003), p. 2.

12 Graham, H. (1993) *Hardship and Health in Women's Lives*, London: Harvester Wheatsheaf.

13 Brynin, M. (1999) 'Smoking behaviour and smoking attitudes', *Journal of Adolescence*, 22, pp. 635-646.

14 Weinstock, M. (2001), Alterations induced by gestational stress

in brain morphology and behaviour of the offspring, *Progress in Neurobiology, 62,* 427-451.

15   O'Connor, T., Heron, J. and Golding, J., Beveridge, M. and Glover, V. (2002), *The British Journal of Psychiatry* 180, pp. 502-508.

16   Hart J. (1971) 'The inverse care law', *Lancet,* 1, pp. 405-412;

17   Rowe and Garcia (2003).

18   Dearden, L., Mesnard, A. and Shaw, J. (2005) *Ethnic differ ences in birth outcomes in England,* London: Institute of Fiscal Studies.

19   Lewis and Drife (2004), cited in Jayaweera, H. *et al.* (2005) 'Pregnancy and childbirth', Dex, S. and Joshi, H. (eds.) *Children of the 21st Century: From birth to nine months,* Bristol: The Policy Press.

20   Page, A. (2002) *Changing Times: Support for Parents and Families During Pregnancy and the First Twelve Months* London: ippr, p. 11

21   Dex, S. and Joshi, H. (2005) *Children of the 21st Century: From birth to nine months,* Bristol: The Policy Press.

22   Jayaweera, H. *et al.* (2005) 'Pregnancy and childbirth', Dex, S. and Joshi, H. (eds.) *Children of the 21st Century: From birth to nine months,* Bristol: The Policy Press, pp. 109-132

23   "The higher risk of lower birth weight for young mothers shown by birth registration statistics disappears once other socio-economic information (primarily housing tenure, car access and Carstairs Deprivation Index) is included in the analysis, which indicates that this effect can be explained by the disadvantaged situation of these mothers."

24   Collingwood Bakeo, A. and Clarke, L. (2006) Risk factors for low birth weight based on birth registration and census informa-tion, England and Wales 1981-2000, p. 21

25   Goodman *et al.* 2004.

26   Shouls, S. *et al.* (1999) *The health and socio-economic circum*

stances of British lone mothers over the last two decades,
Population Trends pp. 41-46.

27   Office National Statistics (2004) *Social Trends 34,* HMSO.

28   UNICEF (2007) *Child poverty in perspective: An overview of*
child well-being in rich countries, Innocenti Report Card 7,
Florence: UNICEF Innocenti Research Centre.

29   Dex and Joshi (2005), p. 113.

30   Of the families surveyed in the Millennium Cohort Study, new
mothers aged 30 and over were almost twice as likely to be
married or living with a partner than new mothers under 20
(92 per cent compared to 47 per cent).

31   In the MCS, only 16% of women aged under 20 and 40% of
those aged 20-24 said their pregnancy was planned, in
contrast to 63 % of women aged 25 to 29 and 70% of women
aged 30 to 34.

32   Jayaweera (2005).

Chapter 4

1   In cases where a diagnosis of Intra-Uterine Growth Retardation
(IUGR) is made, the pregnancy will need to be closely monitored, with frequent clinical check ups and serial ultrasound
scans, as well as biochemical studies and tests to rule out chro-
mosomal therapies and infections. Although there is no proven
effective therapy for IUGR to date, therapies can be adminis-
tered to treat certain foetal infections (such as Toxoplasmosis),
provided an early diagnosis and prompt treatment is possible.
Pregnant women who are diagnosed with IUGR will also be
advised to avoid over-exertion, while undernourished mothers
will be advised to adopt a healthy and nutritious diet.
Importantly, even though the effects of restricted foetal growth
may not be seen until a later stage of pregnancy, nutritious diet
needs to start as early in pregnancy as possible, since studies
have shown that maternal health and nutrition in the early

stages has a better impact on foetal growth than just antenatal supplementation.

2   Page, A. (2002) Changing Times: Support for Parents and Families During Pregnancy and the First Twelve Months, London: ippr.

3   'Cautious welcome to maternity report', Response of the Royal College of Midwives to the report on reconfiguration of maternity services by the National Clinical Director for Children Young People and Maternity Services, Sheila Shribman. Available at:
http://www.rcm.org.uk/news/pages/newsView.php?id=259

4   Shribman, S. (2007) *Making it Better: For Mother and Baby, Clinical case for change*, London: Department of Health.

5   Shribman (2007), p. 7.

6   The smallest babies (those born weighing less than 1000 g) and those born very early (under 28 weeks gestation) will require specialist and intensive medical care, including breathing support, in a Level 3 unit.Those babies who require breathing support, but not intensive care, will be appropriately placed in a Level 2 unit, which offers high dependency care, while Level 1 units are suitable for babies who need less intensive forms of medical care. British Association of Perinatal Medicine (BAPM) (2001) *Standards for Hospitals providing Neonatal Intensive and High Dependency Care*.

7   Robinson, E. (2006) *Weigh less, worth less? A study of neonatal care in the UK*. Bliss Baby Report 2, London: Bliss.

8   Medical guidelines state that neonatal units should not be working at more than 70% occupancy, in order to allow for peaks in demand, for example, in the arrival of triplets (BAPM 2001, p.2).

9   While some transfers are appropriate and will always need to take place on medical grounds (for example, if a baby's condition deteriorates and she needs to be transferred from lower

level units to intensive care), a transfer is *in*appropriate if it takes place because of other constraints – such as lack of capacity – rather than medical need (Robinson 2006, p. 13).

10   Robinson (2006), p. 9

11   This analysis is based on a survey of all neonatal units in the UK, with a 64% response rate, along with a survey of all network managers in England, with a 100% response rate (NPEU 2006).

12   Robinson (2006)

13   Page (2002)

14   Walker (1989)

Chapter 5

1   Recent public information leaflets issued by the Department of Health include a booklet on alcohol use, entitled *'How much is too much: Drinking and you'*, which explains the effects of alcohol on people's health and on their social, home and work life. (DH 2006).

2   For example, the Department of Health recently produced a package of materials for health professionals, entitled 'Obesity Care Pathway and Your Weight, Your Health',(Central Office of Information for the Department of Health, 2006)

3   Rowe, R. and Garcia, J. (2003) *Access to Care for Low Income Childbearing Women: Evidence on Access to Maternity and Infant Care in England*, Oxford University National Perinatal Epidemiology Unit (NPEU) and Maternity Alliance.

4   Sutton, C., Utting, D. and Farrington, D. (2004) Support from the Start: Working with young children and their families to reduce the risks of crime and anti-social behaviour, DfES Research Report 524, London: Department for Education and Skills, p. 15.

5   For example, Professor Michael Crawford argues that the Health Development Agency and Department of Health have not yet

funded the work that would test for a difference: "All studies have been of the 'look-and-see' type and underpowered. The one big study by Rush in New York that is frequently quoted as being unsuccessful if not damaging was done with butter fat as a calorie source along with cow's protein" (personal correspon dence).

6 *Healthy Start* replaced the Welfare Food Scheme in 2002, following a review by the Committee on Medical Aspects of Food and Nutrition Policy (COMA).

7 *Citizens Advice Bureau* (2002) Healthy start promise rings hollow for poorest mothers and children, *www.citizensadvice.org.uk*

8 Green, K. (2005) Getting welfare rights back on the agenda, *Chartist – for democratic socialism*, September 05, http://www.chartist.org.uk/articles/econsoc/sept05green.htm. This conditionality for low-income groups can be contrasted with the use of conditionality for universal benefits. In Finland, for example, every expectant mother is entitled to a govern ment maternity grant (from the 22nd week of pregnancy), providing that she has a health checkup at a prenatal clinic or doctor's surgery before the end of the fourth month of preg- nancy.

9 Sutton, C., Utting, D. and Farrington, D. (2004) Support from the Start: Working with young children and their families to reduce the risks of crime and anti-social behaviour, DfES Research Report 524, London: Department for Education and Skills.

10 Rankin, J. and Regan, S. (2004) *Meeting Complex Needs: The Future of Social Care*, London: Turning Point & IPPR.

11 Cabinet Office (2006) *Reaching Out: An Action Plan on Social Exclusion*, London: Cabinet Office.

12 www.nursefamilypartnership.org.

13 A summary of findings from the Nurse Family Partnership

programme are available on the website: www.nursefamily
partnership.org.

14   Goodman, A. (2006) *The Story of David Olds and the Nurse
        Home Visiting Programme*, Robert Wood Johnson Foundation.
        http://www.rwjf.org/files/publications/other/DavidOldsSpecial
        Report0606.pdf
15   Cabinet Office (2003), pp. 52-55.
16   Cabinet Office (2003), p. 53.

Chapter 6

1   Marmot, M. (2004) *Status Syndrome: How Your Social Standing
        Directly Affects Your Health,* London: Bloomsbury; Wilkinson, R.
        (2005) *The Impact of Inequality: How to make sick societies
        healthier*, London: Routledge.
2   Mayhew, E. and Bradshaw, J. (2005) Mothers, babies and the
        risks of poverty, *Poverty*, 121, pp. 13-16;
        CPAG (2007) *Comprehensive spending review 2007: What it
        needs to deliver on child poverty.* Available at:
        http://www.cpag.org.uk/info/briefings_policy/CSR_2007/
        CSR_2007_6.htm#notes
3   Child Poverty Action Group (2006) *Welfare Benefits & Tax
        Credits Handbook 2006-7*, 8th edition, London: CPAG.
4   Burchett, H. and Seeley, A. (2003) *Good enough to eat? The
        diet of pregnant teenagers*, London: Maternity Alliance and
        Food Commission.
5   For young women aged between 16 and 17 years of age, the
        level of benefit depends on whether they can prove that special
        circumstances apply in their case, such as estrangement from
        parents.
6   Jayaweera, H. *et al.* (2005) Pregnancy and childbirth, in Dex, S.
        and Joshi, H. (eds.) *Children of the 21st Century: From birth to
        nine months*, Bristol: The Policy Press.
7   Importantly, the energy required for the development of these

systems depends on the energy and nutrients in the mother's circulation, and around the lining of the womb. In addition, as the placenta is not yet formed, there is no mechanism to protect the embryo from deficiencies in the mother's circulation, which means that it is even more important that women should have access to a healthy and varied diet in the early stages of pregnancy and also prior to conception.

8   End Child Poverty responds to these objections by proposing the creation of an effectively new pregnancy benefit, which would be equal in rate to child benefit, but which would be paid to the mother not the unborn child, once pregnancy is confirmed.

9   Food Commission (2001) *Children's Nutrition Action Plan Policy recommendations to improve children's diets and health,* Available at: http://www.foodcomm.org.uk/PDF%20files/ Childrens_Nutrition_Action_Plan.pdf

10   Fabian Commission on Life Chances and Child Poverty (2006) *Narrowing the Gap,* London: Fabian Society.

11   CPAG calculate that the value of the adult payments in income support has diminished since it was first introduced in 1988: if income support as a proportion of average earnings had remained the same over time, couples and single adults aged over 25 would have received an extra £33.51 and £22.69 each week in 2005 than was actually the case. CPAG (2007) *Comprehensive spending review 2007: What it needs to deliver on child poverty.* Available at: http://www.cpag.org.uk/info/briefings_policy/CSR_2007/ CSR_2007_6.htm#notes

12   No clear relationship exists at present between benefit levels and what constitutes an adequate level of income to meet minimum living standards (i.e. to meet basic needs such as a healthy diet and decent housing). Although recent research into minimum income standards at the Centre for Research in

Social Policy and the Family Budget Unit has built up a powerful body of evidence about minimum required incomes, this research is not currently being used to determine benefit levels, and there has been no official assessment of the levels needed for individuals and families to live on.

13   Harker, L. (2006) *Delivering on Child Poverty: what would it take?* A report for the Department of Work and Pensions. Available at:http://www.dwp.gov.uk/publications/dwp/2006/harker/harker-full.pdf

14   Bradshaw, J. *et al.* (2005) Socio-economic origins of parents and child poverty, in Dex, S. and Joshi, H. (eds.) *Children of the 21st Century: From birth to nine months*, Bristol: The Policy Press, p. 87.

Chapter 7

1   For instance, in *Our Healthier Nation: A Contract for Health*, Department of Health, January 1998.

2   Social Exclusion Unit (1999) *Teenage Pregnancy: Report to the Prime Minister*, London: HMSO.

3   More recent developments to the government's Teenage Pregnancy Strategy are set out in two documents: *Teenage Pregnancy Next Steps* and *Accelerating the Strategy to 2010*, published by DfES in July and September 2006 respectively.

4   Goodman, A., Kaplan, G. and Walker, I. (2004) *Understanding the Effects of Early Motherhood in Britain: the Effects on Mothers*, London: Institute for Fiscal Studies, p. 28.

5   Teenage Pregnancy Research Programme Briefing (2003) *The Education of Pregnant Young Woman and Young Mothers in England*, London: Department of Health, p2.

6   Goodman *et al.* 2004, p. 28.

7   Berrington *et al.* (2004) *Consequences of Teenage Parenthood, Pathways Which Minimise The Long Term Negative Impacts of Teenage Childbearing*, Southampton: University of

Southampton.

8   For example, high profile media coverage in the mid-nineties
         of a series of tragedies involving children (including the
         murders of Jamie Bulger and the headteacher Philip Lawrence)
         triggered a wave of anxiety over the apparent breakdown of
         traditional institutions and values (e.g. marriage, the family and
         respect for the law). As David Hargreaves (1994) observes, it
         was inevitable that schools would be held responsible in a two-
         edged way: blamed for failing to instil sound moral values,
         whilst at the same time exhorted by government to remove
         such deviancy from the system (The Observer 25 June 1995).

9   Personal correspondence.

10   34.6/1000 in 2001 to 31.5 in 2001, according to ONS figures
         on conception rates. Teenage conceptions, ONS, 2001-2004.

11   Howard Stoate and Bryan Jones (2006), *Challenging the
         Citadel*, London: Fabian Society.

12   Hosie, A. (2001) *A comparative exploration of social policy
         relating to teenage pregnancy in Finland and Scotland,*
         Unpublished doctoral thesis, Stirling: University of Stirling.

13   Finland has 19.4/1000 births to teenagers aged 18-19, in
         1998, compared to 51.8 in the UK (Innocenti)

14   Department of Education and Skills (2005) *Schools and Pupils
         in England 2005*, London: DfES/ONS.

15   Scottish teenage pregnancy expert Dr Alison Hosie remarks
         that while provision for younger parents has improved consid-
         erably in the recent period, there is a striking difference in the
         support available for young people before and after pregnancy.
         In Hosie's view, it is a shame that the same level of support is
         not available earlier, as it would help reduce rates of teenage
         pregnancy, as well as improving young people's health
         outcomes and life chances more generally. It follows that we
         need to look at the kinds of support – financial, educational,
         emotional, relationship etc. – that are available to young

people more widely, particularly those at greatest risk of
becoming a parent in their teens.

16   Page, A. (2002) Changing Times: Support for Parents and
     Families During Pregnancy and the First Twelve Months
     London: ippr, p. 3.

17   Singh and Newburn 2000, cited in Page 2002.

18   Page 2002, p. 9.

19   Dex, S. and Joshi, H. (2005) *Children of the 21st Century:
     From birth to nine months*, Bristol: The Policy Press, p. 7.

20   Bewley, S. *et al*, (2005), 'Which career first? Women caught in
     dilema.', *British Medical Journal*, 331, pp. 588-9; Comment
     (13/09/2006), *Daily Mail*, p. 12.

21   http://www.webpollcentral.com/v2/?id=29496</a>&user=Tig

22   Dixon and Margo 2006, p. 85.

23   Dixon and Margo 2005, p. 86.

24   Dex and Joshi 2005; ONS 2004.

25   Bradshaw *et al* 2005, Castles 2002, Esping-Andersen 1999,
     d'Addio and d'Ercole 2005, Sleebos 2003, cited in Dixon and
     Margo 2006, p. 36.

26   Dixon and Margo 2006.

27   Dixon and Margo 2006.

28   Laroque and Salanié 2003, cited in Dixon and Margo 2006, p.
     37.

29   Green, H. and Parker, S. (2006) *The Other Glass Ceiling: The
     domestic politics of parenting*, London: DEMOS

30   Department for Education and Skills (2002) *The Future of
     Higher Eduction*, London: DfES

31   We might note that the Government's own target on increasing
     university participation amongst people under the age of 30 to
     50 per cent may be unhelpful in this regard.

THE NORTHERN COLLEGE
LIBRARY

95046   BARNSLEY